Pleasure in Reading Aloud and Retelling

Anthony P. Newell   Takane Yamaguchi

KINSEIDO

Kinseido Publishing Co., Ltd.
3-21 Kanda Jimbo-cho, Chiyoda-ku,
Tokyo 101-0051, Japan

Copyright © 2019 by Anthony P. Newell
　　　　　　　　　Takane Yamaguchi

All rights reserved. No part of this publication may be reproduced, stored in a retrieval system, or transmitted, in any form or by any means, electronic, mechanical, photocopying, recording or otherwise, without the prior permission of the publisher.

First published 2019 by Kinseido Publishing Co., Ltd.

Cover design　sein
Text design　　guild
Illustrations　　Minoru Kimura

Song [p.43] JASRAC 出 1809945-801
YOU ARE MY SUNSHINE
Words & Music by Jimmie H. Davis
©1940 by PEER INTERNATIONAL Corp.
International copyright secured. All rights reserved.
Rights for Japan administered by PEERMUSIC K.K.

音声ファイル無料ダウンロード

この教科書で 🎧 DL 00 の表示がある箇所の音声は、上記 URL または QR コードにて
無料でダウンロードできます。自習用音声としてご活用ください。

▶ PC からのダウンロードをお勧めします。スマートフォンなどでダウンロードされる場合は、
　ダウンロード前に「解凍アプリ」をインストールしてください。
▶ URL は、検索ボックスではなくアドレスバー (URL 表示欄) に入力してください。
▶ お使いのネットワーク環境によっては、ダウンロードできない場合があります。

🔘 CD 00　左記の表示がある箇所の音声は、教室用 CD（Class Audio CD）に収録されています。

Preface

Teachers and students of English these days find themselves faced with a huge variety of textbooks to choose from, all emphasizing to one degree or another such skills as reading, writing, listening, and conversing. Here, however, we hope to offer something slightly unusual: a book that encourages learners of English not only to read passages aloud but also to retell them in their own words. These rewarding activities are supplemented by a useful range of others that focus on such things as checking facts, warming up, and working in pairs.

The value of reading aloud is well known. It encourages greater mastery of the target language's sound system and helps learners to recognize and internalize new words and phrases by bringing them to life. The further activity of retelling brings benefit to learners by reinforcing what has been newly learned and serves to give a satisfying sense of accomplishment in the language. The impact of these activities is amplified by making them as enjoyable as possible, and this is reflected in the title of the book, with its emphasis on the *pleasure* that can be gained from approaching English in this way.

I would like to offer my sincere thanks to my editor, Ms. Michi Tsutahara, whose patience and support have been indispensable in carrying the book through to its successful completion, and to my co-author, Professor Takane Yamaguchi, whose skill and imagination in devising useful and effective tasks have made such an important contribution to this book.

Anthony P. Newell

Pleasure in Reading Aloud and Retelling は、音読という活動を通して、英文の内容と音声を能動的に習得するためのテキストです。音読は英語上達に効果があると言われていますが、本テキストではその効果をより高めるための様々な工夫を盛り込みました。例えば、各章の導入部は絵を使った語彙問題や簡単なリスニング活動を通して、みなさんが興味を持ってパッセージ読解へと進めるように作られています。300語程度のパッセージを読んだ後には、"通じる" 英語の音読法をペアワークで学んでいきます。パッセージの意味内容に応じた強弱のつけ方やイントネーションに注意を向けることで、単純に声を出すだけにとどまらない英語らしい読み方を習得します。各章のまとめでは、音読から一歩進んで、読んだ内容を自分の言葉で再現してみる Retelling（リテリング）という活動を取り入れました。外国語でまとまった内容を話すことは容易ではありませんが、習得した言葉にメッセージを吹き込むという活動は、非常に効果的な英語学習法であり、言語学習の醍醐味でもあります。各章で学んできたことを総動員して取り組んでみてください。

最後になりますが、声に出して読んでみたくなる彩り豊かな15のパッセージをご執筆くださった Anthony P. Newell 先生に、心より感謝申し上げます。

山口 高領

本書の構成と使い方

音読活動を効果的に行うには、英文の意味を正確につかみ、さらにその音声や内容・表現を学習者が自分のものとして取り込むという姿勢が大切です。そのような学習を助けるために、本書では音読活動にとどまることなく、音声や表現を能動的・多角的に学ぶためのエクササイズを豊富に用意しました。

各ユニットは6ページ構成で、導入→英文読解→音読活動という流れで展開します。

▶ pp.6～8「音読トレーニングの心得」「リテリングのコツ」を学習してから本編に入ると効果的です。

導入

Picture Dictionary
メインの英文に登場するフレーズを、イラストを使って視覚的に学びます。ここで学んだフレーズは、英文読解やユニットの終わりのリテリングのセクションで役立ちます。

Fact Checker
英文の題材に関する背景知識や事実情報を、ディクテーションで学びます。短い文章や表、詩などを通して、これから読む英文により親しみを持てるよう工夫してあります。

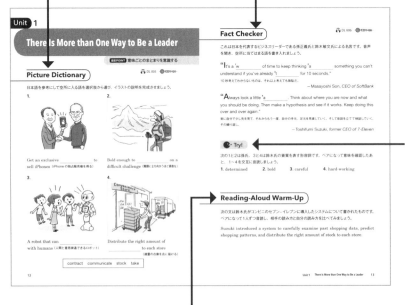

Try!
重要語句やアクセントを確認するセクションです。ペアで単語やフレーズ、短い文を発音し、音読活動に入る前の準備をします。

Reading-Aloud Warm-Up
メインの英文から抜き出された文をペアで音読し、相手の読み方と自分の読み方を比べます。後のセクションで詳細に学ぶ英文ですので、まずは気軽に声に出してみましょう。

英文読解

Reading
300語程度で書かれたメインの英文を読みます。なるべく日本語を介さず、物語の流れを意識して読みましょう。

Check!
パラグラフごとに内容を短時間で確認できる練習問題です。

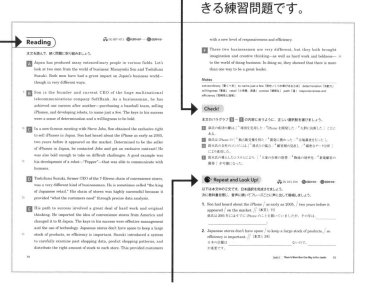

Repeat and Look Up!
2つの英文の意味を確認した後、教科書を閉じてフレーズごとに暗唱する活動です。次の音読活動でも取り上げる英文ですので、ここでしっかりと「意味」と「音」を習得しましょう。

音読活動

Reading Aloud
英文から1つのパラグラフに焦点を当て、英語音声の特徴を詳細に学びます。ハイライトされた英文には 音読POINT として解説があり、英語らしく読むためのコツを紹介しています。最後に、Check Points! をもとにペアで評価しあいます。

Retelling the Story
Reading Aloud とは違うパラグラフに焦点を当て、その内容を自分の言葉で再現するリテリングの活動をします。まず Picture Dictionary で登場した2つのイラストを見ながらもう一度音声を聞き、内容を思い出した後で、ヒントを参考にしながら内容を再現していきます。これまでに学んできたことを総括するつもりで、取り組んでみましょう。

音読トレーニングの心得　3か条

音読トレーニングをする際に大切な3つのポイントです。各ユニットの音読活動の際に意識をすると効率的です。

❶ 意味ごとのまとまりを意識する！　　DL 002　CD1-02

英語の文を読むときは**センス・グループ**（意味ごとのまとまり）を意識することが大切です。各フレーズの意味内容を理解したうえで、どこでセンス・グループを区切ればよいか考えてみましょう。一例として、以下のスラッシュが入った場所で区切られることが多いです。

例：①Unlike dogs, / cats have never been completely tamed. //
　　②I think / that our plan will succeed / in the long run. //
　　③People around the world / are interested in Japan / —④its culture, / its historical sites, / its food, / and its beautiful landscapes. //

▶ ①前置詞句・副詞句の後や、②長めの目的語の前、③長めの主語の後、④並列されている複数の要素の間など、スラッシュが入ることが多い場所を押さえ、そこにポーズを入れて読んでみましょう。慣れてきたら、ポーズの長さを短くして読んでみてもよいでしょう。

❷ 強弱をつけて、リズムに乗って読む！　　DL 003　CD1-03

英語ではすべての単語が同じ強さで読まれるのではなく、強弱をつけて読まれます。
一般的に、**内容語**（実質的な意味を持つ語：名詞、動詞、形容詞、副詞、疑問詞など）は強く読まれ、**機能語**（文法上の機能を持つ語：助動詞、前置詞、代名詞、接続詞など）は弱く読まれる傾向にあります。

例：I **ho**pe you **li**ke it.
　　Why are **peo**ple so **in**terested in **see**ing **cats**?

▶ 内容語が強く読まれ、その他の語は弱めに読まれます。上では、内容語の中で第一強勢（アクセント）が来る場所を太字と•で示しました。•がほぼ等間隔になるようなイメージで、リズムに乗って発音してみましょう。

❸ 音のつながり・弱く読まれる子音に注意する！ 🎧 DL 004 💿 CD1-04

英語では、単語の語尾と次の単語の頭がつながる現象が起こることがあります。音のつながりを意識すれば、なめらかに読めるようになります。
また、子音を読むときは弱めに読み、母音が入らないように気をつけましょう。

例： There was a cup on the table, but I broke it.
　　 Did you believe in Santa Claus when you were a child?

▶ p, t, d, k, s, r, m, n などの子音のあとに母音または y の音が続く場合、音がつながる傾向が強いです。

例： Ted put the newspaper on the desk.
　　 Tim likes strolling along the street in spring.

▶ p, t, d, k, g などの子音が文末に来たときや、似た音の前に来たとき、弱く発音され、聞こえなくなることがあります。例えば put の語末は「ト」と母音を入れずに、/t/ を軽く添えるように読みましょう。/t/ の音は非常に弱く、喉に手を当てても声帯が震えない「無声音」と呼ばれる音です。

以上の3か条を基準に、自分の音読を意識的にモニターすることが大切です。
どの段階でも、すべて上手にできていなくても心配ありません。また、必ずしもネイティブのような速さで読む必要もありません。相手にしっかり伝わるように、自分自身で「意識」しながら読むことで、一歩ずつ上達していきましょう。

音読記号一覧

本書の Reading Aloud のセクションでは、以下の記号を用いて読み方の例を示しています。
（一部みなさんが実際に記号を書き入れる活動も取り入れています）

記号	意味	記号	意味
/	ポーズを入れる（文末は //）	[ ]	まとまりを意識して
ho**pe**	強く読む※	→	後に続くように
‿	音をつなげる	↘	下げて
Japan	はっきり、ゆっくりめに	↗	上げて

※本書では基本的に、内容語の第一強勢が来る音節を太字にしています。ただし、機能語でも強く読まれる場合は第一強勢の音節を太字にしています。

リテリング（再話）のコツ

音読に慣れてきたら、今度は読んだ内容を相手に伝える練習をしてみましょう。ある内容を自分なりに要約して相手に伝えることを Retelling（リテリング＝再話）と呼びます。この練習を繰り返すことで、まとまった情報を効果的に伝える能力が身につきます。

Unit 5 を例に、Retelling のやり方を学びましょう。次の英文は、ロシアのウラジオストクにおける人気の見所を紹介しています。これを「自分の言葉で」再現するにはどうしたらよいでしょうか。

There are many interesting things to see in Vladivostok. The most popular is probably the huge and impressive bridge that links the city with Russky Island. It is the longest bridge of its type in the world—just the central section is more than one kilometer in length....

英文を再現するときのポイントは、元の文を一字一句正確に言う必要はなく、内容を要約して短くしたり、別の言葉に置き換えたりしてもよいという点です。ここでは、「ウラジオストクで最も人気なのは〜です」と、まず結論を簡潔に述べる手法を使ってみましょう。
▶ The most popular spot in Vladivostok is _____.

あなたなら、空所に何を入れて読みますか？本文のとおり、the huge and impressive bridge that links the city with Russky Island と言ってもよいですが、より簡潔に、the huge bridge や、the very large and impressive bridge などと言い換えても構いません。
さらに情報を追加したいときは、It links Vladivostok with Russky Island. や、It is the longest bridge of its type in the world! などと続けて言うこともできます。

大切なのは完璧に言うことではなく、情報を取捨選択し、本文の言葉と自分の言葉を織り交ぜながら「語る」ことです。
本書では、各章のまとめとして Retelling の練習を取り入れています。クラスメイトと一緒に、自分の言葉で語り、情報を共有する楽しみを味わいましょう！

Table of Contents

本書の構成と使い方 ……………………………………………………………… 4

音読トレーニングの心得　3か条 ………………………………………………… 6

リテリング（再話）のコツ ……………………………………………………… 8

Unit 1 **There Is More than One Way to Be a Leader** ………… 12
　　　　音読POINT 意味ごとのまとまりを意識する

Unit 2 **A Cool Response to Food Waste** ……………………… 18
　　　　音読POINT 内容語と機能語を意識する

Unit 3 **Haiku—Having Fun with Words and Ideas** ………… 24
　　　　音読POINT 弱い子音の読み方

Unit 4 **Could Your Face Cost You Your Privacy?** …………… 30
　　　　音読POINT つながる音の読み方

Unit 5 **Russia's City of the East** ……………………………… 36
　　　　音読POINT 補足情報と強調情報の読み方

Unit 6 **The Healing Power of Music** ………………………… 42
　　　　音読POINT 逆接から主張を導く

Unit 7 **Looking at Life through the Eyes of a Cat** ………… 48
　　　　音読POINT 対比情報に注意して読む

| Unit 8 | **Designing Solutions to Everyday Problems** | 54 |

音読POINT 疑問文のイントネーション

| Unit 9 | **Currying Favor in Britain and Japan** | 60 |

音読POINT 並列情報の読み方

| Unit 10 | **Interacting with Others in a Globalized World** | 66 |

音読POINT 数字情報の読み方

| Unit 11 | **The Tragedy of Rana Plaza** | 72 |

音読POINT 核心から詳細を述べる

| Unit 12 | **The Age of Innocence** | 78 |

音読POINT 感情を込めて読む

| Unit 13 | **Kiribati: A Paradise on Earth— But for How Much Longer?** | 84 |

音読POINT 他の人の発言を紹介する

| Unit 14 | **Two Great Painters…and a Stormy Friendship** | 90 |

音読POINT メッセージの中心を際立たせる

| Unit 15 | **What's in a Name?** | 96 |

音読POINT 複雑な文構造を読む

Unit 1

There Is More than One Way to Be a Leader

音読POINT 意味ごとのまとまりを意識する

DL 005 CD1-05

Picture Dictionary

日本語を参考にして空所に入る語を選択肢から選び、イラストの説明を完成させましょう。

1.

Get an exclusive _____ to sell iPhones（iPhone の独占販売権を得る）

2.

Bold enough to _____ on a difficult challenge（難題に立ち向かうほど勇敢な）

3.

A robot that can _____ with humans（人間と意思疎通できるロボット）

4.

Distribute the right amount of _____ to each store （適量の在庫を店に届ける）

| contract   communicate   stock   take |

Fact Checker

これは日本を代表するビジネスリーダーである孫正義氏と鈴木敏文氏による名言です。音声を聞き、空所に当てはまる語を書き入れましょう。

"It's a ¹w_____ of time to keep thinking ²a_____ something you can't understand if you've already ³t_____ for 10 seconds."

10秒考えてわからないものは、それ以上考えても無駄だ。

—Masayoshi Son, *CEO of SoftBank*

"Always look a little ⁴a_____. Think about where you are now and what you should be doing. Then make a hypothesis and see if it works. Keep doing this over and over again."

常に自分で少し先を見て、それからもう一度、自分の手元、足元を見直していく。そして仮説を立てて検証していく。その繰り返し。

—Toshifumi Suzuki, *former CEO of 7-Eleven*

次の1と2は孫氏、3と4は鈴木氏の資質を表す形容詞です。ペアになって意味を確認したあと、1〜4を交互に音読しましょう。

1. determined　　2. bold　　3. careful　　4. hard-working

Reading-Aloud Warm-Up

次の文は鈴木氏がコンビニのセブン-イレブンに導入したシステムについて書かれたものです。ペアになって1人ずつ音読し、相手の読み方と自分の読み方を比べてみましょう。

Suzuki introduced a system to carefully examine past shopping data, predict shopping patterns, and distribute the right amount of stock to each store.

Reading

本文を読んで、続く問題に取り組みましょう。

A　Japan has produced many extraordinary people in various fields. Let's look at two men from the world of business: Masayoshi Son and Toshifumi Suzuki. Both men have had a great impact on Japan's business world—though in very different ways.

B　Son is the founder and current CEO of the huge multinational telecommunications company SoftBank. As a businessman, he has achieved one success after another—purchasing a baseball team, selling iPhones, and developing robots, to name just a few. The keys to his success were a sense of determination and a willingness to be bold.

C　In a now-famous meeting with Steve Jobs, Son obtained the exclusive right to sell iPhones in Japan. Son had heard about the iPhone as early as 2005, two years before it appeared on the market. Determined to be the seller of iPhones in Japan, he contacted Jobs and got an exclusive contract! He was also bold enough to take on difficult challenges. A good example was his development of a robot—"Pepper"—that was able to communicate with humans.

D　Toshifumi Suzuki, former CEO of the 7-Eleven chain of convenience stores, was a very different kind of businessman. He is sometimes called "the king of Japanese retail." His chain of stores was highly successful because it provided "what the customers need" through precise data analysis.

E　His path to success involved a great deal of hard work and original thinking. He imported the idea of convenience stores from America and changed it to fit Japan. The keys to his success were effective management and the use of technology. Japanese stores don't have space to keep a large stock of products, so efficiency is important. Suzuki introduced a system to carefully examine past shopping data, predict shopping patterns, and distribute the right amount of stock to each store. This provided customers with a new level of responsiveness and efficiency.

F These two businessmen are very different, but they both brought imagination and creative thinking—as well as hard work and boldness—to the world of doing business. In doing so, they showed that there is more than one way to be a great leader.

Notes

extraordinary「驚くべき」 to name just a few「例をいくつか挙げるならば」 determination「決断力」 willingness「意欲」 retail「小売業、流通」 precise「綿密な」 path「道」 responsiveness and efficiency「即時性と効率」

Check!

本文のパラグラフ **B** ~ **E** の内容に合うように、正しい選択肢を選びましょう。

B 孫氏の成功の鍵は、[¹ 球団を売却した / ² iPhone を開発した / ³ 大胆に決断した] ことにある。

C 孫氏は iPhone の [¹ 独占販売権を得た / ² 開発に携わった / ³ 市場調査を行った]。

D 鈴木氏の会社のコンビニは、[¹ 孫氏との協力 / ² 顧客層の見直し / ³ 綿密なデータ分析] により成功した。

E 鈴木氏の導入したシステムにより、[¹ 大量の在庫の保管 / ² 物流の効率化 / ³ 新規顧客の獲得] が可能になった。

Repeat and Look Up!

DL 013, 014   CD1-13   CD1-14

以下は本文中の2文です。日本語訳を完成させましょう。
次に教科書を閉じ、音声に続いてフレーズごとに声に出して暗唱しましょう。

1. Son had heard about the iPhone / as early as 2005, / two years before it appeared / on the market. // （本文 l. 11）
   孫氏は2005年にはすでに iPhone のことを聞いていましたが、その年は、_____ _____ 。

2. Japanese stores don't have space / to keep a large stock of products, / so efficiency is important. // （本文 l. 24）
   日本の店舗は _____ ないので、_____ が重要です。

Reading Aloud

鈴木氏の成功の要因について書かれたパラグラフ E を音読してみましょう。

1. まず太字で示された強く読む部分と 音読POINT の文に注意しながら、パラグラフ E の一部を聞きましょう。
   次に、自分でも / と ⌣ の記号（詳細は p.6）を書き込んでみましょう。

   DL 015　CD1-15

The **keys** to his suc**cess** were ef**fec**tive **man**agement and the **use** of tech**nol**ogy. Japa**nese stores** don't have **space** to **keep** a **large stock** of **prod**ucts, so ef**fic**iency is im**por**tant. 音読POINT Suzuki intro**duced** a **sys**tem / [to **care**fully ex**am**ine **past shop**ping **da**ta,] / [pre**dict shop**ping **pat**terns,] / and [dis**trib**ute the **right a**mount of **stock** to **each store**]. //

> **音読POINT** 意味ごとのまとまりを意識する
>
> ポイント文では、a system 以下に 3 つの情報 A, B, and C が並列され、すべて a system を説明しています。[ ] で囲まれた 3 つのまとまりを意識しましょう。A と B の間に軽くポーズを入れ、and C の前には少し長めのポーズを入れましょう。また、1 つのまとまり内ではポーズを入れたりイントネーションを下げたりせずに、一気に読むことを心がけましょう。

2. 最後に、ペアになって上の英文を 1 人ずつ音読し、**Check Points!** をもとに評価しあいましょう。

☑ ***Check Points!***
❶ 強弱を意識し、リズムに乗って読めているか　　　　　　　　　　　　　　　[　　 / 3点]
❷ 書き込んだ通りにポーズ、音のつながりを意識して読めているか　　　　　　[　　 / 3点]
❸ ポイント文について、音読POINT を意識して読めているか　　　　　　　　　[　　 / 3点]

Total Score: 　/ 9点

Retelling the Story

孫氏の成功を物語るエピソードを、自分の言葉で再現してみましょう。

1. まずパラグラフ C をもう一度聞き、下のイラストに関連するキーワードを書き込んでみましょう。

    DL 016　CD1-16

▶ Key Words

(　　　　　　　　　　　　)　　(　　　　　　　　　　　　)

2. 次に、下の英文の下線部を補いながら、孫氏の成功エピソードを2つ紹介しましょう。本文を見ずに、上のキーワードを参考にしたり、本文の表現を思い出したりしながら自分の言葉で話しましょう。

Be Determined and Bold: Son's Success Story

Masayoshi Son achieved one success after another.

エピソード1　In a now-famous meeting with Steve Jobs, Son ＿＿＿＿＿＿
＿＿＿＿＿＿＿＿＿＿＿＿＿＿＿＿＿＿＿＿＿＿＿＿＿＿＿＿＿＿＿＿．

Son had heard about ＿＿＿＿＿＿＿＿＿＿＿＿＿＿＿＿＿＿＿＿＿＿．

エピソード2　He was also bold enough ＿＿＿＿＿＿＿＿＿＿＿＿＿＿．

For example, he developed ＿＿＿＿＿＿＿＿＿＿＿＿＿＿＿＿＿＿＿
＿＿＿＿＿＿＿＿＿＿＿＿＿＿＿＿＿＿＿＿＿＿＿＿＿＿＿＿＿＿＿＿．

Unit 1　There Is More than One Way to Be a Leader

Unit 2

A Cool Response to Food Waste

音読POINT 内容語と機能語を意識する

DL 017　CD1-17

Picture Dictionary

日本語を参考にして空所に入る語を選択肢から選び、イラストの説明を完成させましょう。

1.

Food that is perfectly ＿＿＿＿＿＿
（問題なく食べられる食べ物）

2.

An idea to help ＿＿＿＿＿＿ food waste（フードロスを防ぐためのアイデア）

3.

Put food in or ＿＿＿＿＿＿ food out（食べ物を入れたり取り出したりする）

4.

Give ＿＿＿＿＿＿ food to poor people（貧しい人に無料で食べ物を与える）

---

edible　free　take　prevent

Fact Checker

これは、国連の食糧農業機関が発表している世界のフードロスについての情報です。音声を聞き、空所に当てはまる語を書き入れましょう。

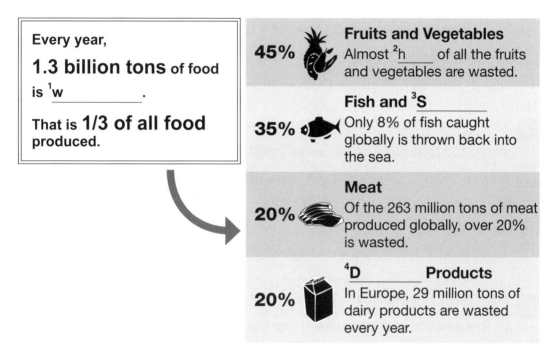

Every year, **1.3 billion tons** of food is ¹w_____.

That is **1/3 of all food** produced.

Fruits and Vegetables — 45%
Almost ²h_____ of all the fruits and vegetables are wasted.

Fish and ³S_____ — 35%
Only 8% of fish caught globally is thrown back into the sea.

Meat — 20%
Of the 263 million tons of meat produced globally, over 20% is wasted.

⁴D_____ Products — 20%
In Europe, 29 million tons of dairy products are wasted every year.

 Try!

次の数字の読み方を確認しましょう。その後、ペアになって1〜4を交互に音読してみましょう。

1. 1.3 billion **2.** 1/3 **3.** 2/3 **4.** 4,500,000

Reading-Aloud Warm-Up

次の文は東京におけるフードロスの現状について書かれたものです。ペアになって1人ずつ音読し、相手の読み方と自分の読み方を比べてみましょう。

Every day in Tokyo alone, the food just thrown away could feed 4.5 million people! The main reason is that customers have unrealistic expectations about food.

Reading

本文を読んで、続く問題に取り組みましょう。

A Have you ever wondered what happens to all the food that supermarkets and restaurants fail to sell? Most of it gets thrown away—even though it's perfectly edible. Believe it or not, some official estimates have suggested that at least 30% of all the food produced globally goes to waste.

B The problem exists in Japan as much as anywhere else. Every day in Tokyo alone, the food just thrown away could feed 4.5 million people! The main reason is that customers have unrealistic expectations about food. They want what manufacturers call "PPP" food: perfect, pristine, and pretty. Anything that is not PPP—even though it's perfectly edible—remains unsold and gets discarded.

C But people in Galdakao, a town in northern Spain, came up with a solution to the problem of food waste. They put a communal fridge in the street. Anyone can put food in it or take food out. "We started to think that if just one garbage can were replaced with a fridge, people could take advantage of these items," said Álvaro Saiz, one of the organizers. He adds that this fridge is not there to give free food to poor people. Instead, it's about the proper use of food. "We must recover the value of food and fight against waste," he says.

D Of course, there are rules to make sure the food in the fridge is safe to eat. No raw meat or fish is allowed, for example, and canned goods must be within their use-by date. So far, there have been no problems. All the food put in has been taken on a daily basis, and all sorts of people have made use of the fridge—including a workman who took an ice cream on a hot

day! All in all, the project has saved hundreds of kilos of food from being wasted.

E In recent years, efforts have been made to cut food waste in Japan, too. It is something that everyone can help with. Would you consider helping, too?

Notes

fail to do「～し損なう」 estimate「推定」 feed「食べ物を与える、養う」 unrealistic expectation「非現実的な期待」 manufacturer「製造者」 pristine「新品の」 discard「捨てる」 communal「共同社会の」 take advantage of「利用する」 proper「適切な」 use-by date「消費期限」 all in all「合計で」

Check!

本文のパラグラフ A ～ D の内容に合うように、正しい選択肢を選びましょう。

A スーパーなどで売れなくなった食べ物の大半は [¹ 安売りされる / ² 廃棄される / ³ リサイクルされる]。

B フードロスの主な理由として、[¹ 製造者の調査不足 / ² 顧客の過大な期待 / ³ 廃棄業者の増加] が挙げられる。

C スペインでの試みは、[¹ 貧しい人へ食べ物を届ける / ² 古い冷蔵庫を有効に活用する / ³ 食品廃棄を減らす] 目的があった。

D 共有冷蔵庫に入れられる食品は、[¹ 毎日のように利用される / ² 肉や魚が中心である / ³ アイスクリームが人気である]。

Repeat and Look Up!

以下は本文中の2文です。日本語訳を完成させましょう。
次に教科書を閉じ、音声に続いてフレーズごとに声に出して暗唱しましょう。

1. Every day in Tokyo alone, / the food just thrown away / could feed 4.5 million people! // (本文 l. 5)
   東京だけでも、毎日捨てられている食料は ＿＿＿＿＿＿＿＿＿＿＿＿＿＿＿＿＿＿＿＿＿＿＿＿＿＿＿＿＿＿＿＿ 。

2. This fridge is not there / to give free food / to poor people. // (本文 l. 15)
   この冷蔵庫は、＿＿＿＿＿＿＿＿＿＿＿＿＿＿＿＿＿＿＿＿＿＿ そこにあるのではありません。

Reading Aloud

フードロスの現状について書かれたパラグラフ B を音読してみましょう。

1. まず太字で示された強く読む部分と 音読POINT の文に注意しながら、パラグラフ B の一部を聞きましょう。
次に、自分でも / と ⌣ の記号（詳細は p.6）を書き込んでみましょう。

 DL 026   CD1-26

Every **day** in **To**kyo a**lone**, the **food** just **thrown** a**way** could **feed 4.5 mil**lion **peo**ple!   音読POINT   The **main rea**son is / that **cus**tomers have unreal**is**tic expec**ta**tions about **food**. // They **want** what manu**fac**turers **call** "PPP" **food**: **per**fect, **pris**tine, and **pret**ty. **An**ything that is **not** P**PP**—even though it's **per**fectly **ed**ible—re**mains** un**sold** and **gets** dis**card**ed.

音読POINT 内容語と機能語を意識して、強弱をつける

太字の語は強めに、それ以外の語は弱めに読むようにしましょう。ポイント文に、「～ということ」という意味の that があります。that の前で軽くポーズを入れたあと、that 自体は軽く添えるように弱く読みます。なお、最後の文の Anything that... の that も弱く読みますが、これは関係代名詞の that なので、前にポーズを入れず一気に読みます。

---

2. 最後に、ペアになって上の英文を1人ずつ音読し、***Check Points!*** をもとに評価しあいましょう。

✓ *Check Points!*
❶ 強弱を意識し、リズムに乗って読めているか　　　　　　　　　　　　　　[　／3点]
❷ 書き込んだ通りにポーズ、音のつながりを意識して読めているか　　　　　[　／3点]
❸ ポイント文について、音読POINT を意識して読めているか　　　　　　　　[　／3点]

Total Score: ／9点

Retelling the Story

スペインのガルダカオで始まった共有冷蔵庫について、自分の言葉で再現してみましょう。

1. まずパラグラフ C をもう一度聞き、下のイラストに関連するキーワードを書き込んでみましょう。

   DL 027   CD1-27

▶ Key Words

(   )

▶ Key Words

(   )

2. 次に、下の英文の下線部を補いながら、共有冷蔵庫のしくみと、その背景にある考え方を紹介をしましょう。本文を見ずに、上のキーワードを参考にしたり、本文の表現を思い出したりしながら自分の言葉で話しましょう。

A Solution to the Problem of Food Waste

People in Galdakao came up with a wonderful idea:

They put _____.

しくみ Anyone could _____.

With a fridge, people _____.

考え方 However, this fridge is not there to _____.

Instead, it's about _____.

One of the organizers said, "_____."

Unit 2　A Cool Response to Food Waste

Unit 3

Haiku—Having Fun with Words and Ideas

音読POINT 弱い子音の読み方

Picture Dictionary

🎧 DL 028　💿 CD1-28

日本語を参考にして空所に入る語を選択肢から選び、イラストの説明を完成させましょう。

1.

Mown grass _____ to shoes（靴にくっつく芝生の草）

2.

Impress the judges of a _____（コンテストの審査員を感心させる）

3.

_____ a line for a haiku（俳句の1行をアップロードする）

4.

Young people in India and _____（インドとパキスタンの若者たち）

| competition　Pakistan　upload　sticking |

Fact Checker

これは株式会社伊藤園主催の第28回『伊藤園お〜いお茶新俳句大賞』英語部門の入賞作品です。音声を聞き、空所に当てはまる語を書き入れましょう。

- **Winner**

  Gracie Starkey, a ¹_____-year-old student at Wycliffe College, in England

- **Work**

  > freshly mown grass
  > clinging to my ²s_____
  > my muddled thoughts

  Notes　cling「くっつく」　muddled「混乱した、はっきりしない」

- **Prize**
  - A cash prize of £1,500 ($2,000) and a copy of the poem in calligraphic form
  - Winning haiku to be featured on the company's ³g_____ ⁴t_____ bottles for a year

Try!

ペアになって上の俳句を交互に読み、日本語の俳句と似ている点と異なる点を話し合ってみましょう。

Reading-Aloud Warm-Up

次の文はイギリスの13歳の少女が俳句を書くきっかけとなった出来事を述べています。ペアになって1人ずつ音読し、相手の読み方と自分の読み方を比べてみましょう。

One day, as she was walking around the school campus, some grass stuck to her shoes. That's what led her to write the poem.

Reading

本文を読んで、続く問題に取り組みましょう。

A The English haiku on the previous page was written by a 13-year-old student in England, Gracie Starkey. One day, as she was walking around the school campus, some grass stuck to her shoes. That's what led her to write the poem. Like all good haiku, it captures a moment in time, an idea, a feeling. It impressed the judges of a haiku competition so much that they chose it as the winning poem.

B Poems in haiku form were first made popular in Japan by great poets like Matsuo Basho, who lived in the 17th century. In his day, the name "hokku" was used, and it was the opening part of a longer poem. Now, however, it is an independent form of poetry. The basic rules of writing an English haiku are simple: Use three lines; keep them short—three or four words per line; and include a seasonal feeling. Writing haiku became popular in the English-speaking world early in the 20th century. Today, schools often use haiku to teach children about poetry.

C Writing haiku continues to grow in popularity, especially online. One app—Haiku Jam—allows someone to write a line of haiku and then upload it. Another person writes the next line in reply. This app has been used for a project for young people in India and Pakistan, two countries that have often had bad relations with each other. Seventy years after these countries became independent, however, the app has provided a way for these young people to work together and have fun at the same time.

D
        united we stand
        divided we fall
        alone we crawl

This is one of the haiku these young people have written. The first two lines help to explain and overcome their differences. The last line shows the danger of not getting along together. Isn't it true that we, as human beings, succeed best when we cooperate with each other?

E A haiku is not difficult to write, but it can contain a surprising idea or a deep message. Perhaps you should try it, too!

30

Notes

capture「とらえる」 independent「独立した」 in reply「返答して」 relations「関係」 united「団結して」 divided「分裂して」 overcome「克服する」 contain「含む」

Check!

本文のパラグラフ A ～ D の内容に合うように、正しい選択肢を選びましょう。

A 前のページに示されている俳句は、[¹ 日本人によって / ² 作者の日常体験をもとに / ³ 学校の宿題の一部として] 作られた。

B 英語の俳句に必要なのは、[¹ 5・7・5のリズム / ² 短く表現すること / ³ 3行か4行で書くこと] である。

C Haiku Jam は、[¹ 俳句の普及 / ² 国を超えた創作行為 / ³ インドの独立運動] に使われた。

D この段落に示されている俳句は、[¹ 両国の良好な関係 / ² 独立運動の失敗 / ³ 協力し合うことの難しさ] を示している。

Repeat and Look Up!

以下の2文は本文中の英文です。日本語訳を完成させましょう。
次に教科書を閉じ、音声に続いてフレーズごとに声に出して暗唱しましょう。

1. Like all good haiku, / it captures a moment in time, / an idea, a feeling. //
   (本文 l. 4)
   多くのよい俳句と同じように、それは _____ をとらえています。

2. This app has been used / for a project for young people / in India and Pakistan, / two countries that have often had / bad relations with each other. // (本文 l. 17)
   このアプリは、インドとパキスタンの若者のためのプロジェクトで使われてきましたが、両国はこれまで _____ 。

Reading Aloud

13歳のイギリスの少女による俳句について書かれたパラグラフ A を音読してみましょう。

1. まず太字で示された強く読む部分と 音読POINT の文に注意しながら、パラグラフ A の一部を聞きましょう。
   次に、自分でも / と ‿ の記号（詳細は p.6）を書き込んでみましょう。

   🎧 DL 037　💿 CD1-37

The **En**glish hai**ku** on the **pre**vious **page** was **writ**ten by a **13**-year-old **stu**dent in **En**gland, **Gra**cie **Star**key. 音読POINT **One day**, / as she was **walk**ing around the **school cam**pus, / some **grass stuck** to her **shoes**. // That's what **led** her / to **write** the **po**em. // Like **all good** hai**ku**, it **cap**tures a **mo**ment in **time**, an i**dea**, a **feel**ing.

音読POINT 弱い子音の読み方

ポイント文で下線が引かれた語は弱く読まれる子音です。語末に来る子音は、日本語の around「アラウンド」のように母音を入れるのでなく、軽く添えるように読みましょう。また、grass stuck など、後に同じ音が来る場合は、先行する s の音がほとんど聞こえなくなることもあります。grass や stuck のように語頭に子音の連結がある場合も、語頭に母音を入れずに一気に読むよう心がけましょう。

---

2. 最後に、ペアになって上の英文を1人ずつ音読し、*Check Points!* をもとに評価しあいましょう。

☑ ***Check Points!***
❶ 強弱を意識し、リズムに乗って読めているか　　　　　　　　　　　[　／3点]
❷ 書き込んだ通りにポーズ、音のつながりを意識して読めているか　　[　／3点]
❸ ポイント文について、音読POINT を意識して読めているか　　　　　[　／3点]

Total Score: ／9点

Retelling the Story

俳句リレーのためのアプリ Haiku Jam について、自分の言葉で再現してみましょう。

1. まずパラグラフ C をもう一度聞き、下のイラストに関連するキーワードを書き込んでみましょう。

▶ Key Words
( )

▶ Key Words
( )

2. 次に、下の英文の下線部を補いながら、Haiku Jam について、概要に具体例を加えて説明しましょう。本文を見ずに、上のキーワードを参考にしたり、本文の表現を思い出したりしながら自分の言葉で話しましょう。

What is Haiku Jam?
概要の説明 In an app called Haiku Jam, someone _____ _____. Then, another _____ _____.
具体例 This app has been used for a project for _____ _____.   They work together making haiku and _____.

Unit 4

Could Your Face Cost You Your Privacy?

音読POINT つながる音の読み方

DL 039　CD1-39

Picture Dictionary

日本語を参考にして空所に入る語を選択肢から選び、イラストの説明を完成させましょう。

1.

A _____ the police are trying to catch（警察が捕まえようとしている犯人）

2.

A customer paying for her _____（購入品の支払いをする客）

3.

_____ faces in social network profiles（SNS上で顔を特定する）

4.

Be _____ as they enter the shop（入店時に撮影される）

photographed　criminal　purchases　identify

Fact Checker

これは中国の情報通信業の中心的存在である、アリババグループの導入したシステムの写真と説明文です。音声を聞き、空所に当てはまる語を書き入れましょう。

Alibaba's "smile to pay" facial recognition system

Imaginechina/JIJI

A resident of Zhengzhou, in China, ¹p_____ for her medicine at a pharmacy ²v_____ Alipay's self-service system, which offers a facial-recognition service. The "future drugstore" enables people to use a 24-hour self-service system that ³s_____ ⁴d_____ and other services.

Note Zhengzhou「鄭州市（中国の河南省の省都）」

Try!

上の英文を参考にして、次の日本語の意味に合うように空所を埋めましょう。その後、どこにアクセントが来るかに注意して、ペアになって1と2を交互に音読してみましょう。

1. 顔認証　　（　　　　　　　　） recognition
2. 未来の薬局　future (　　　　　　　)

Reading-Aloud Warm-Up

次の文は中国で取り入れられている支払いシステムについて書かれています。ペアになって1人ずつ音読し、相手の読み方と自分の読み方を比べてみましょう。

In some stores in China, for example, you can already "pay with a smile" using FRT and its link to your bank account. This is certainly a convenient way of paying.

Reading

本文を読んで、続く問題に取り組みましょう。

A For a long time, we have been identified by things like our fingerprints, our teeth, and our DNA. But technology that uses the uniqueness of our faces, too, has now been developed. It's called Facial Recognition Technology, or FRT. What are the advantages of this recent development?

B There are three main points. First, it helps the police to catch criminals. Using FRT in public places like railway stations and streets, the police can find people they are looking for. Secondly, it can be used in shops to let customers pay for their purchases. In some stores in China, for example, you can already "pay with a smile" using FRT and its link to your bank account. This is certainly a convenient way of paying. Thirdly, it can be used to help us access our phones and our computers. This technology adds a level of security that is not offered by having just a password or key.

C But, as with all types of technology, there may be cause for concern. For one thing, FRT is a risk to our privacy. A Russian app called FindFace, for example, can identify faces in photos and link them automatically to social network profiles, thus naming the people in the photos. In supermarkets, shoppers can be photographed and identified as they enter. The supermarket can then change the price of its goods based on the shopper's identity, using digital price labels instead of paper labels. And what about your boss? He or she could now use FRT to monitor where you go and what you do. Your privacy would disappear.

D FRT is already here. Like all technology, it has both good and bad points. What is your opinion? Are you happy to allow your face to be recognized wherever you go? Or will you feel like wearing a face mask every time you go shopping?

Notes

identify「身元を特定する」 fingerprint「指紋」 criminal「犯罪者」 bank account「銀行口座」
concern「懸念」 automatically「自動的に」 feel like doing「～したいと思う」

Check!

本文のパラグラフ A ～ D の内容に合うように、正しい選択肢を選びましょう。

A 身元の特定のために、[¹ 指紋はそれほど有効ではない / ² 顔認証技術が開発されている / ³ DNA 鑑定はもっとも信頼できる]。

B 顔認証技術の利点には、[¹ 犯罪者の捜索が容易になる / ² 銀行口座が不要になる / ³ パスワードを覚えやすい] 点がある。

C 顔認証技術の応用の際に懸念されることは、[¹ いじめの増加 / ² 犯罪の増加 / ³ 個人情報の流出] だ。

D 顔認証技術は [¹ 日本では発達しないだろう / ² 長所も短所もある / ³ マスクの着用を促すだろう]。

Repeat and Look Up!

DL 045, 046   CD1-45   CD1-46

以下は本文中の2文です。日本語訳を完成させましょう。
次に教科書を閉じ、音声に続いてフレーズごとに声に出して暗唱しましょう。

1. Using FRT in public places / like railway stations and streets, / the police can find people / they are looking for. // （本文 l. 6）
   警察は、＿＿＿＿＿＿＿＿＿＿＿＿＿＿＿＿＿＿ などの公共の場で顔認証技術を使って、＿＿＿＿＿＿＿＿＿＿＿＿＿＿＿＿＿＿ ことができます。

2. In supermarkets, / shoppers can be photographed / and identified / as they enter. // （本文 l. 16）
   スーパーでは、買い物客は入店時に＿＿＿＿＿＿＿＿＿＿＿＿＿＿＿＿＿＿＿＿＿＿＿＿＿＿＿＿＿。

Reading Aloud

顔認証技術の利便性について書かれたパラグラフ B を音読してみましょう。

1. まず太字で示された強く読む部分と 音読POINT の文に注意しながら、パラグラフ B の一部を聞きましょう。
   次に、自分でも / と ⌣ の記号（詳細は p.6）を書き込んでみましょう。

   DL 047   CD1-47

First, it **helps** the po**lice** to **catch crim**inals. U**s**ing FRT in **pub**lic **place**s like **rail**way **sta**tions and **streets**, the po**lice** can **find peo**ple they are **look**ing for. **Sec**ondly, it can be **used** in **shops** to **let cus**tomers **pay** for their **pur**chases. 音読POINT In **some stores** in **Chi**na, / for e**xam**ple, / you can al**read**y ["**pay** with a **smile**"] / **us**ing FRT / and its **link** to your **bank** ac**count**. // This is **cer**tainly a con**ven**ient **way** of **pay**ing.

音読POINT つながる音の読み方

子音で終わる単語のあとに母音で始まる単語が続くとき、音がつながる現象が起こることがあります。Unit 1 で学んだように、意味ごとのかたまり（特に pay with a smile や bank account などのフレーズ）は一気に読まれ、語と語の間隔が必然的に短くなりますから、結果的に音がつながって聞こえます。また、and its などの機能語は弱く、速く縮めて読まれることから、機能語どうしがつながる現象もよく起こります。

2. 最後に、ペアになって上の英文を1人ずつ音読し、*Check Points!* をもとに評価しあいましょう。

✓ *Check Points!*
❶ 強弱を意識し、リズムに乗って読めているか　　　　　　　　　　　　　[　　/3点]
❷ 書き込んだ通りにポーズ、音のつながりを意識して読めているか　　　　[　　/3点]
❸ ポイント文について、音読POINT を意識して読めているか　　　　　　　[　　/3点]

Total Score:　/9点

Retelling the Story

顔認証技術の懸念点について、自分の言葉で再現してみましょう。

1. まずパラグラフ C の一部をもう一度聞き、下のイラストに関連するキーワードを書き込んでみましょう。

 DL 048　 CD1-48

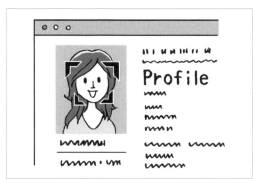

▶ Key Words　　　　　　　　　　▶ Key Words

(　　　　　　　　　　　)　　(　　　　　　　　　　　)

2. 次に、下の英文の下線部を補いながら、顔認証技術の2つの懸念点を述べてみましょう。本文を見ずに、上のキーワードを参考にしたり、本文の表現を思い出したりしながら自分の言葉で話しましょう。

Concern over Facial Recognition Technology

FRT has many advantages, but it can also be a risk to our privacy.

懸念点1　For example, a Russian app called _____

_____.

懸念点2　In supermarkets, shoppers can _____

_____.

The data may be used by the supermarket to change _____

_____.

Unit 4　Could Your Face Cost You Your Privacy?

Unit 5

Russia's City of the East

音読POINT 補足情報と強調情報の読み方

Picture Dictionary

日本語を参考にして空所に入る語を選択肢から選び、イラストの説明を完成させましょう。

1.

Good things like _____ and caviar（バレエやキャビアなど肯定的なもの）

2.

A bridge that _____ the city with an island（街と島をつなぐ橋）

3.

A _____ station of classical European design（古典的な欧風様式の鉄道駅）

4.

Asian food _____ in popularity（人気の高まるアジア料理）

growing　links　ballet　railway

Fact Checker

これはロシアの主要都市と近隣諸国との位置関係を示した地図です。音声を聞き、空所にあてはまる都市名を選択肢から選び、地図内に書き入れましょう。

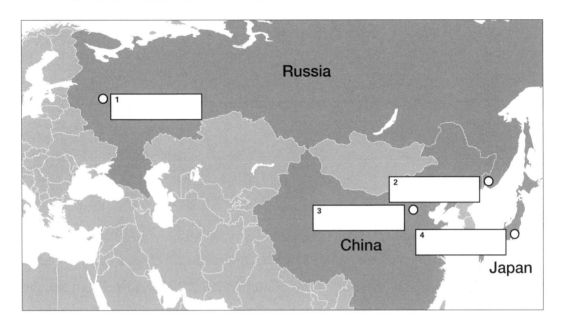

Tokyo　Beijing　Vladivostok　Moscow

 Try!

次の地名の強く発音される部分に印をつけましょう。その後、ペアになって1~3を交互に発音してみましょう。

1. Beijing　　**2.** Moscow　　**3.** Vladivostok

Reading-Aloud Warm-Up

次の文はウラジオストクの位置について書かれています。ペアになって1人ずつ音読し、相手の読み方と自分の読み方を比べてみましょう。

This port city is just three hours by plane from Tokyo. It's even closer to China—just about 60 kilometers from China's eastern border.

Reading

本文を読んで、続く問題に取り組みましょう。

A　When you think of Russia, what image comes to mind? Do you think of positive things like ballet, great novels, and caviar? Or do you think of more negative stereotypes, such as spies and gangsters? Although Russia is one of Japan's closest neighbors, the fact is that most Japanese are not very familiar with the country or its people. So what might be interesting to Japanese travelers?

B　As a matter of fact, the nearest large Russian city to Japan is the city of Vladivostok. This port city—Russia's most important in the east—is just three hours by plane from Tokyo. It's even closer to China—just about 60 kilometers from China's eastern border. But although it is so close to China and Japan, its atmosphere is not really Asian. The architecture and the people are much more likely to remind visitors of Europe.

C　There are many interesting things to see in Vladivostok. The most popular is probably the huge and impressive bridge that links the city with Russky Island. It is the longest bridge of its type in the world—just the central section is more than one kilometer in length.

D　Another spot worth visiting is the main railway station. Its gorgeous architecture and the huge, beautiful pictures on the walls give visitors a real feeling of classical European design. This station is at one end of the world-famous Trans-Siberian Railway, which links Vladivostok with the capital, Moscow. The capital is over 9,000 kilometers away—so even if you never get off the train, it still takes about a week to get there!

E　What about the people? Even though Vladivostok is in the Far East, most of the citizens look European and, of course, they speak Russian in their daily lives. However, many of the cars they drive are second-hand cars from Japan, and Asian food is growing in popularity. This influence from the surrounding region is one of the things that make Vladivostok a unique city—a place that is well worth visiting.

Notes

novel「小説」 atmosphere「雰囲気」 architecture「建築物」 remind ~ of...「~に…を思い起こさせる」
second-hand「中古の」 influence「影響」 surrounding「周囲の」 region「地域」

Check!

本文のパラグラフ B ~ E の内容に合うように、正しい選択肢を選びましょう。

B ウラジオストクは [¹中国よりも日本に近い / ²東京から3時間で行ける / ³アジアの雰囲気を持っている]。
C ウラジオストクの大きな橋は、[¹中国とロシア / ²日本とロシア / ³島と街] をつなぐ。
D ウラジオストク駅からシベリア鉄道に乗ると、[¹北京 / ²モスクワ / ³ロシア国外] に行くことができる。
E ウラジオストクでは [¹英語が日常的に使われている / ²日本の中古車を見かける / ³欧風の食事がおいしい]。

Repeat and Look Up!

以下の2文は本文中の英文です。日本語訳を完成させましょう。
次に教科書を閉じ、音声に続いてフレーズごとに声に出して暗唱しましょう。

1. Although it is so close / to China and Japan, / its atmosphere is not really Asian. // (本文 l. 10)
   それは中国や日本のとても近くにありますが、＿＿＿＿＿＿＿＿＿＿＿＿＿＿＿＿＿＿＿
   ＿＿＿＿＿＿＿＿＿＿＿＿＿＿＿＿＿＿＿＿。

2. The most popular is probably / the huge and impressive bridge / that links the city with Russky Island. // (本文 l. 13)
   もっとも人気が高いのはおそらく、ルースキー島と＿＿＿＿＿＿＿＿＿＿＿＿＿＿＿＿＿
   ＿＿＿＿＿＿＿＿＿＿＿＿＿＿＿＿＿＿＿。

Reading Aloud

ウラジオストクの位置について書かれたパラグラフ B を音読してみましょう。

1. まず太字で示された強く読む部分と 音読POINT の文に注意しながら、パラグラフ B の一部を聞きましょう。
   次に、自分でも / と ⌣ の記号 (詳細は p.6) を書き込んでみましょう。

   🎧 DL 058　💿 CD1-58

As a **mat**ter of **fact**, the **near**est **large Rus**sian **ci**ty to Ja**pan** is the **ci**ty of Vladi**vo**stok. 音読POINT This **port ci**ty / —**Rus**sia's **most** im**por**tant in the **east**— / is **just three hours** by **plane** / from **To**kyo. // It's **e**ven **clos**er to **Chi**na—just about **60 ki**lometers from **Chi**na's **east**ern **bor**der. But al**though** it is so **close** to **Chi**na and Ja**pan**, its **at**mosphere is **not re**ally **A**sian.

> **音読POINT 補足情報と強調情報の読み方**
>
> This port city を Russia's most important in the east が補足しています。このような補足情報の前では、軽くポーズを置くとよいでしょう。日本語で言う「つまり」の意味が—（ダッシュ）に含まれています。This port city のあとにイントネーションを下げすぎないようにして、後に続きがあることも意識しましょう。また、この文で一番大切な情報は文の終盤にある three hours の部分です。just の前で軽く息継ぎをし、three hours を強調しましょう。

2. 最後に、ペアになって上の英文を1人ずつ音読し、*Check Points!* をもとに評価しあいましょう。

☑ *Check Points!*

❶ 強弱を意識し、リズムに乗って読めているか　　　　　　　　　　　　[　/3点]
❷ 書き込んだ通りにポーズ、音のつながりを意識して読めているか　　　[　/3点]
❸ ポイント文について、音読POINT を意識して読めているか　　　　　　[　/3点]

Total Score:　/9点

Retelling the Story

ウラジオストクの見所について、自分の言葉で再現してみましょう。

1. まずパラグラフ C と D の一部をもう一度聞き、下のイラストに関連するキーワードを書き込んでみましょう。

   DL 059　CD1-59

▶ Key Words　　　　　　　　　　▶ Key Words

(　　　　　　　　　　　　)　　(　　　　　　　　　　　　)

2. 次に、下の英文の下線部を補いながら、ウラジオストクの2つの見所を紹介してみましょう。本文を見ずに、上のキーワードを参考にしたり、本文の表現を思い出したりしながら自分の言葉で話しましょう。

Interesting Things to See in Vladivostok

There are many _____ in Vladivostok.

見所① The most popular is _____

_____.

見所② Another spot worth visiting is _____.

Its gorgeous architecture and the beautiful pictures on the walls give

_____.

Unit 6

The Healing Power of Music

音読POINT 逆接から主張を導く

Picture Dictionary

DL 060　CD1-60

日本語を参考にして空所に入る語を選択肢から選び、イラストの説明を完成させましょう。

1.

_____ sick people with flute music（フルートで病人を癒す）

2.

Make us more positive and less _____ （より前向きにして不安を減らす）

3.

Use music _____ for cancer patients（ガン患者に音楽療法を採用する）

4.

Have the power to _____ the brain（脳を刺激する力を持つ）

| anxious　therapy　stimulate　treat |

Fact Checker

これはアメリカで古くから親しまれている人気曲 *You Are My Sunshine* の歌詞の一部です。歌詞を聞き、空所に当てはまる語を書き入れましょう。

You are my sunshine, my only sunshine

You make me ¹h_____ when skies are ²g_____

You'll never know dear, ³h_____ much I love you

Please don't take my sunshine ⁴a_____

—Words and Music by Jimmie H. Davis

上の歌を聞いた人は、一般的にどのような気持ちになるでしょうか。当てはまると思う形容詞を下からすべて選びましょう。その後、ペアになって1～4を交互に発音してみましょう。

1. anxious　　**2.** positive　　**3.** stressed　　**4.** powerful

Reading-Aloud Warm-Up

次の文は音楽を聞くことの意味について書かれています。ペアになって1人ずつ音読し、相手の読み方と自分の読み方を比べてみましょう。

We listen to music because we enjoy it. However, some people are interested in music for a different reason—its effect on health.

Reading

本文を読んで、続く問題に取り組みましょう。

A Music is an aspect of human culture that we find all over the world. Its origins may have been artistic or religious: or perhaps people made music simply for pleasure. That is how most of us regard it today—we listen to it because we enjoy it.

B However, some people are interested in music for a different reason—its effect on health. This idea is not a new one. Two thousand years ago, the ancient Greeks wrote about treating sick people with flute music. Now, though, scientists and doctors are using modern technology to study the effect of music on our bodies.

C Evidence has shown that music has a positive effect in two main ways. One is that music can improve our mood and frame of mind, making us more positive and less anxious. This approach to helping patients has been adopted, for example, at Mount Sinai Brooklyn, a hospital in New York. There, doctors use music therapy for people anxious about their cancer. The doctors find it works so well that a patient's level of stress and anxiety can drop by as much as 20%.

D There is also a biological side: music seems to have the power to stimulate the brain and encourage the release of powerful natural chemicals. One of these is dopamine, a chemical involved in our perception and experience of pleasure. It can also have an effect on chronic pain. Studies have shown that people suffering from pain can find physical relief by listening to certain types of music. So it is not just that the music helps to take our mind off pain—the sound actually helps our bodies to produce chemicals that act toward relieving it.

E As evidence of these benefits grows, it may feature more and more in medical treatments of the future. From now on, when you listen to music, keep in mind that it is not just fun to listen to—it may also be good for your health!

Notes

aspect「側面」 religious「宗教的な」 frame of mind「心持ち」 adopt「採用する」 anxiety「不安」
biological「生物学的な」 dopamine「ドーパミン（脳細胞が作りだす神経伝達物質の一種）」
perception「知覚」 chronic pain「慢性的な痛み」 relieve「取り除く」 feature「重要な役割を果たす」

Check!

本文のパラグラフ A ～ D の内容に合うように、正しい選択肢を選びましょう。

A 私たちの多くは音楽を [¹ 宗教的なもの / ² 楽しみのために聞くもの / ³ もっともすばらしい芸術] と見なしている。

B 音楽の健康への影響は [¹ 古代ローマで / ² 現代の研究で / ³ 若者たちの間で] 解明されようとしている。

C ある病院で採用された音楽療法は [¹ 病気の症状 / ² 病気への不安な気持ち / ³ 動物のストレス] を軽減した。

D 音楽には [¹ 体の痛みを和らげる / ² 人に共感する気持ちを高める / ³ ドーパミンの働きを抑える] 効果がある。

Repeat and Look Up!

DL 067, 068　CD1-67　CD1-68

以下は本文中の2文です。日本語訳を完成させましょう。
次に教科書を閉じ、音声に続いてフレーズごとに声に出して暗唱しましょう。

1. Two thousand years ago, / the ancient Greeks wrote / about treating sick people with flute music. // （本文 l. 6）
   2,000年前、古代ギリシア人は＿＿＿＿＿＿＿＿＿＿
   書き記しています。

2. It was found / that a patient's level of stress and anxiety / can drop by as much as 20%. // （本文 l. 15、一部改変）
   患者のストレスと＿＿＿＿＿＿＿＿＿＿
   ことがわかりました。

Reading Aloud

音楽を聞く意味について書かれたパラグラフ A B を音読してみましょう。

1. まず太字で示された強く読む部分と 音読POINT の文に注意しながら、パラグラフ A の最終文と B を聞きましょう。
   次に、自分でも / と ⌣ の記号（詳細は p.6）を書き込んでみましょう。

   DL 069　CD1-69

音読POINT We **lis**ten to **mu**sic / be**cause** we en**joy** it. // How**ev**er, / some **peo**ple are **in**terested in **mu**sic / for a **dif**ferent **rea**son / —its ef**fect** on **health**. // This i**dea** is **not** a **new** one. **Two thou**sand **years** a**go**, the **an**cient **Greeks wrote** about **treat**ing **sick peo**ple with **flute mu**sic. **Now**, though, **sci**entists and **doc**tors are **us**ing **mod**ern tech**nol**ogy to **stud**y the ef**fect** of **mu**sic on our **bod**ies.

音読POINT　逆接から主張を導く

「音楽は楽しむもの」という一般的に受け入れられている事実を述べてから、「楽しむ以外の理由があるんですよ…」という話し手の伝えたい主張に移っています。However「けれども」は話題を転換し、後ろにくる内容を際立たせる役目があるので、はっきり、ゆっくりめに読みます。2文目の最後が最も言いたいことなので、for a different reason の後では長めのポーズを取り、聞き手に興味を抱かせ、its effect on health に焦点が当たるように読みましょう。

---

2. 最後に、ペアになって上の英文を1人ずつ音読し、**Check Points!** をもとに評価しあいましょう。

✓ Check Points!
❶ 強弱を意識し、リズムに乗って読めているか　　　　　　　　　　　[　　/3点]
❷ 書き込んだ通りにポーズ、音のつながりを意識して読めているか　　[　　/3点]
❸ ポイント文について、音読POINT を意識して読めているか　　　　[　　/3点]

Total Score:　/9点

Retelling the Story

音楽が精神に与える効能について、自分の言葉で再現してみましょう。

1. まずパラグラフ C をもう一度聞き、下のイラストに関連するキーワードを書き込んでみましょう。

   DL 070   CD1-70

▶ Key Words
( )

▶ Key Words
( )

2. 次に、下の英文の下線部を補いながら、ニューヨークのある病院で発見された音楽の効能を紹介してみましょう。本文を見ずに、上のキーワードを参考にしたり、本文の表現を思い出したりしながら自分の言葉で話しましょう。

Evidence of the Good Effect of Music

Music can improve _____
_____.

ある病院での発見 This approach has been adopted at Mount Sinai Brooklyn, a hospital in New York. There, doctors use _____
_____.

It was found that _____
_____.

Unit 6　The Healing Power of Music

Unit 7

Looking at Life through the Eyes of a Cat

音読POINT 対比情報に注意して読む

DL 071　CD1-71

Picture Dictionary

日本語を参考にして空所に入る語を選択肢から選び、イラストの説明を完成させましょう。

1.

_____ a cat at the cat's own eye level（ネコの目の位置で撮影する）

2.

A photo showing both a cat and its _____ （ネコと周囲を撮った写真）

3.

A _____ with cats shared by many（多くの人に共有されるネコへの心酔）

4.

An animal that has been _____ （飼いならされてきた動物）

| fascination | film | surroundings | tamed |

Fact Checker

これは動物写真家の岩合光昭さんのプロフィールです。音声を聞き、空所に当てはまる語を書き入れましょう。

Quick Facts

- **Name**   Iwago Mitsuaki
- **Occupation** Wildlife ¹p_____
- **Born**   November 27, ²_____
- **Birthplace** Tokyo, Japan
- **Early Life** Began photographing animals ³f_____ a trip to the Galapagos Islands
- **Major Works** Best-selling photo books
                  An NHK TV ⁴s_____ called "It's a Cat's Life"

©Iwago Photographic Office

 Try!

次の各単語のもっとも強く発音される部分に印をつけましょう。その後、ペアになって1〜4を交互に発音してみましょう。

1. wildlife　　**2.** photographer　　**3.** islands　　**4.** best-selling

Reading-Aloud Warm-Up

次の文はイヌや人間と対比したネコの特徴を述べたものです。ペアになって1人ずつ音読し、相手の読み方と自分の読み方を比べてみましょう。

Why are people so interested in seeing cats? For one thing, unlike dogs, cats have never been completely tamed. They share a world shaped by humans, but in many ways they make it their own.

Reading

DL 073~076　CD1-73 ~ CD1-76

本文を読んで、続く問題に取り組みましょう。

A Sometimes it's good to look at life in a different way and get a fresh view of things. That is what the photographer Iwago Mitsuaki has done. Best known for his work with wildlife, Iwago developed an interest in photographing animals following a trip with his father to the Galapagos Islands. He has since traveled the world to capture the lives of animals on film. His work is good enough to have appeared in globally influential magazines like *National Geographic*.

B In recent times, Iwago has made a series for television called "It's a Cat's Life." From Okinawa to France, Iwago has filmed cats in different natural surroundings. His work has three distinct features that make it special.

C First, he always tries to film a cat at the cat's own eye level, seeing what the cat sees, not what we as humans are used to seeing. Second, he shows both cats and their surroundings in a way that is interesting, as well as representative of a cat's life. As a result, his images often have the quality of beautiful paintings, moments captured forever. Typical of this is one image of a cat sitting among falling cherry blossom. Finally, he approaches cats with respect and patience, waiting to become accepted into their world, rather than imposing himself on it. This lets him see things others miss.

D His work shows a fascination with cats that is shared by many. Why are people so interested in seeing cats? For one thing, unlike dogs, cats have never been completely tamed. They share a world shaped by humans, but in many ways they make it their own. So the character of each

cat comes out as it explores the world and adapts to its surroundings. As Iwago shows, this can sometimes be funny, surprising, or sad. Perhaps that reassures us, as our own lives can be funny, surprising, and sad. Iwago's cats can be our connection back to nature. By watching his films about cats, we see our own world afresh.

Notes

capture「とらえる」 influential「影響力のある」 distinct「際立った」 representative「代表している」
patience「忍耐」 impose「押し付ける」 adapt to「〜に馴染む」 reassure「安心させる」

Check!

本文のパラグラフ A 〜 D の内容に合うように、正しい選択肢を選びましょう。

A 岩合さんは主に [¹ ガラパゴス諸島の動物 / ² 世界中の動物 / ³ ナショナルジオグラフィック誌向け] の写真を撮っている。

B 岩合さんの作品は [¹ 絶景を背景に撮影されている / ² 沖縄からフランスに行く間で作られた / ³ テレビで放送された]。

C 岩合さんの作品の特徴は [¹ 絵と見分けがつかない / ² 春の季節が中心である / ³ ネコの世界観を捉えようとしている] ことだ。

D ネコの姿を見ることで、私たちは [¹ イヌの習性 / ² 新しい世界の見方 / ³ 世界を変える方法] を知ることができる。

Repeat and Look Up!

DL 077, 078   CD1-77   CD1-78

以下の2文は本文中の英文です。日本語訳を完成させましょう。
次に教科書を閉じ、音声に続いてフレーズごとに声に出して暗唱しましょう。

1. He approaches cats / with respect and patience, / waiting to become accepted into their world, / rather than imposing himself on it. //
（本文 l. 16）
彼は尊敬と忍耐をもってネコに接し、＿＿＿＿＿＿＿＿＿＿＿＿＿＿＿＿＿、
ネコの世界に自らを押し付けることはしません。

2. Why are people so interested / in seeing cats? // （本文 l. 20）
人々はなぜ＿＿＿＿＿＿＿＿＿＿＿＿＿＿＿＿＿＿＿＿＿＿＿＿＿＿＿＿＿。

Reading Aloud

ネコの魅力について書かれたパラグラフ D を音読してみましょう。

1. まず太字で示された強く読む部分と 音読POINT の文に注意しながら、パラグラフ D の一部を聞きましょう。
   次に、自分でも / と ⌣ の記号（詳細は p.6）を書き込んでみましょう。

🎧 DL 079   💿 CD1-79

Why are **peo**ple so **in**terested in **see**ing **cats**? 音読POINT For **one** thing, / unlike **dogs**, / **cats** have **nev**er been com**plete**ly **tamed**. // They **share** a **world shaped** by **hu**mans, / [but in **many** ways] / they **make** it **their own**. // So the **char**acter of **each cat** comes **out** as it ex**plores** the **world** and a**dapts** to its sur**round**ings. As **Iwa**go **shows**, this can **some**times be **fun**ny, sur**pris**ing, or **sad**.

音読POINT 対比情報に注意して読む

ポイント文ではイヌや人間と対比したネコの特徴が述べられます。never been completely tamed と make it their own の部分は特にゆっくりはっきり読みましょう（cats を表す their は機能語ですが、対比効果を出すためにここでは強く読みます）。これらの内容を際立たせるために、unlike dogs や shaped by humans の後にポーズをやや長めに取り、息継ぎをしてから読みましょう。

---

2. 最後に、ペアになって上の英文を1人ずつ音読し、**Check Points!** をもとに評価しあいましょう。

☑ *Check Points!*
❶ 強弱を意識し、リズムに乗って読めているか　　　　　　　　　　　　　[　　/ 3点]
❷ 書き込んだ通りにポーズ、音のつながりを意識して読めているか　　　　[　　/ 3点]
❸ ポイント文について、音読POINT を意識して読めているか　　　　　　[　　/ 3点]

Total Score: [　　/ 9点]

Retelling the Story

岩合光昭さんの写真の特徴について、自分の言葉で再現してみましょう。

1. まずパラグラフ C をもう一度聞き、下のイラストに関連するキーワードを書き込んでみましょう。

　　　　　　　　　　　　　　　　　　　　　　　🎧 DL 080　　💿 CD1-80

▶ Key Words　　　　　　　　　　　▶ Key Words

(　　　　　　　　　　　　)　　　(　　　　　　　　　　　　)

2. 次に、下の英文の下線部を補いながら、岩合さんの写真の３つの特徴を語ってみましょう。本文を見ずに、上のキーワードを参考にしたり、本文の表現を思い出したりしながら自分の言葉で話しましょう。

What Makes Iwago's Photos Special?

His work has three distinct features that make it special.

| 特徴1 | First, he always tries to _____ .

| 特徴2 | Second, he shows _____
_____ .

| 特徴3 | Finally, he approaches cats with respect and patience, waiting to
_____ .

Unit 8
Designing Solutions to Everyday Problems

音読POINT 疑問文のイントネーション

Picture Dictionary

DL 081　CD1-81

日本語を参考にして空所に入る語を選択肢から選び、イラストの説明を完成させましょう。

1.

The job of a design _____
（デザイン・エンジニアの仕事）

2.

A vacuum cleaner that often gets
_____（よく詰まる掃除機）

3.

_____ cyclone power to the design of a vacuum cleaner
（サイクロンの力を掃除機の設計に応用する）

4.

_____ for engineers in Japan （日本におけるエンジニアへの尊敬）

```
respect    engineer    blocked    apply
```

Fact Checker

以下はデザイン・エンジニアという仕事の説明と、イギリスのデザイン・エンジニアであるジェームズ・ダイソン氏の言葉です。音声を聞き、空所に当てはまる語を書き入れましょう。

What do "design engineers" do?

Design engineers use technical knowledge and design skills to create ¹i_____ ²s_____ to everyday problems and make people's lives better.

Design is only truly beautiful when it ³w_____ ⁴p_____.
—James Dyson

©K.Murata/©Kazutoshi Murata

Try!

次の各単語のもっとも強く発音される部分に印をつけましょう。その後、ペアになって1〜4を交互に音読しましょう。

1. engineer
2. technical
3. innovative
4. properly

Reading-Aloud Warm-Up

次の文はデザイン・エンジニアの仕事のイメージについて書かれています。ペアになって1人ずつ音読し、相手の読み方と自分の読み方を比べてみましょう。

Now, what's your image of design engineering? Do you think it would be a nice job to have? Young people in Britain don't seem to think so.

Unit 8　Designing Solutions to Everyday Problems

Reading

本文を読んで、続く問題に取り組みましょう。

A Machines are a big part of our daily lives—smartphones, fridges, microwave ovens, and so on. But before any machine can be made, someone must sit down and work out exactly how it will work and what it will look like. That is the job of an engineer.

B There are different sorts of engineers, one of which is known as a design engineer. A very successful example is James Dyson, who comes from Britain. His approach to engineering is to find everyday problems in a machine that people are already using and then reinvent it in a completely different way. The secret of his success lies in two key points.

C The first is frustration. Take vacuum cleaners, for example. He once bought one of the most powerful vacuum cleaners on the market. But before long, it got blocked, and the dust bags started losing their power to pick up dust. His feeling of frustration made him want a better vacuum cleaner. The challenge was how to make one.

D That brings us to the second key point—ingenuity. Dyson came up with brilliant solutions that no one else had thought of. One day, he was at a local sawmill and noticed how the sawdust was being removed from the air by large cyclones. He applied this cyclone power to the design of a vacuum cleaner. As a result, the vacuum cleaner he invented didn't need dust bags, so it didn't lose its suction power over time. His ingenious invention soon became very popular.

E Dyson has produced a string of innovative inventions that not only work well, but are pleasing to look at. Now, what's your image of design engineering? Do you think it would be a nice job to have? Young people in Britain don't seem to think so—the number of British youngsters who want to be engineers is falling. Worried about this, Dyson talked about it in an interview: "Here in Britain, we don't seem to have the respect for engineers that people in Japan and China have. We have a choice: Do we want Britain to be a theme park or a hub of creative engineering?" He is keen to inspire young people to become involved in this important field.

Notes

lie in「〜にある」 frustration「不満、イライラ」 ingenuity「創意工夫」 sawmill「製材所」 sawdust「おがくず」 suction power「吸引力」 a string of「一連の」 hub「(活動の)中心」 keen「熱心な」

Check!

本文のパラグラフ A C D E の内容に合うように、正しい選択肢を選びましょう。

A どんな機械でも、作る前に、[¹ 機能性と見た目 / ² 座り心地のよさ / ³ 売上の見込み] について考える必要がある。

C ダイソンは、[¹ 顧客の声 / ² 自らの体験 / ³ 若い頃の挫折] によって、よりよい掃除機を作りたいと思った。

D ダイソンが作った掃除機は、[¹ メンテナンスが不要だった / ² 巨大な集塵袋を備えていた / ³ 集塵袋が不要だった]。

E ダイソンは [¹ イギリスのエンジニアの未来 / ² イギリスの娯楽産業 / ³ 日本のエンジニアの労働環境] について心配している。

Repeat and Look Up!

DL 088, 089   CD1-88   CD1-89

以下の2文は本文中の英文です。日本語訳を完成させましょう。
次に教科書を閉じ、音声に続いてフレーズごとに声に出して暗唱しましょう。

1. He applied this cyclone power / to the design of a vacuum cleaner. //
   (本文 l. 18)
   彼はサイクロンの力を _____。

2. Dyson has produced / a string of innovative inventions / that not only work well, / but are pleasing to look at. // (本文 l. 22)
   ダイソンは機能性がすぐれているだけでなく、_____
   _____ を生み出してきました。

Reading Aloud

エンジニアの仕事のイメージについて書かれたパラグラフ E を音読してみましょう。

1. まず太字で示された強く読む部分と 音読POINT の文に注意しながら、パラグラフ E の一部を聞きましょう。
   次に、自分でも / と ⌒ の記号（詳細は p.6）を書き込んでみましょう。

   🎧 DL 090 💿 CD1-90

Dyson has pro**duc**ed a **string** of **in**novative in**ven**tions that **not only work well**, but are **pleas**ing to **look** at. 音読POINT Now, / what's your **im**age / of de**sign** engi**neer**ing? // Do you **think** / it would be a **nice job** to **have**? // Young **peo**ple in **Brit**ain **don't seem** to **think** so—the **num**ber of **Brit**ish **young**sters who **want** to be engi**neers** is **fall**ing.

音読POINT 疑問文のイントネーション

一般的に、What, When, How などの疑問詞で始まる疑問文は、文末を下降調のイントネーションで読みます。Do you...? / Are you...? などの Yes/No 疑問文は、多くの場合上昇調になります。疑問文は会話文だけでなく、スピーチやプレゼンなどでも効果的に用いられます。上の例でも、2つの疑問文を投げかけることで、聞き手が話題について考えるための「間」を与えています。疑問文のあとの間を大切にして読みましょう。

---

2. 最後に、ペアになって上の英文を1人ずつ音読し、*Check Points!* をもとに評価しあいましょう。

✓ *Check Points!*

❶ 強弱を意識し、リズムに乗って読めているか　　　　　　　　　　　　　　[　／3点]
❷ 書き込んだ通りにポーズ、音のつながりを意識して読めているか　　　　　[　／3点]
❸ ポイント文について、音読POINT を意識して読めているか　　　　　　　　 [　／3点]

Total Score: ／9点

Retelling the Story

ダイソン氏がデザイン・エンジニアとして成功した要因を、自分の言葉で再現してみましょう。

1. まずパラグラフ C D をもう一度聞き、下のイラストに関連するキーワードを書き込んでみましょう。

DL 091　CD1-91

▶ Key Words

(　　　　　　　　　　　　)

▶ Key Words

(　　　　　　　　　　　　)

2. 次に、下の英文の下線部を補いながら、ダイソン氏の成功要因を2つ紹介してみましょう。本文を見ずに、上のキーワードを参考にしたり、本文の表現を思い出したりしながら自分の言葉で話しましょう。

Dyson's Keys to Success as a Design Engineer

The secret of Dyson's success lies in two key points.

要因1　The first is _____ . A vacuum cleaner he once bought often got _____ .

This feeling of frustration made him _____ .

要因2　That brings us to the second key point, _____ .

He found brilliant solutions. By applying _____ ,

he invented a cleaner that _____ .

Unit 9

Currying Favor in Britain and Japan

音読POINT 並列情報の読み方

Picture Dictionary

DL 092　CD2-02

日本語を参考にして空所に入る語を選択肢から選び、イラストの説明を完成させましょう。

1.

Curry recipes _____ in Britain（イギリスで広まるカレーのレシピ）

2.

British _____ who brought curry to Japan（日本にカレーを伝えた英国貿易商）

3.

Taste buds not _____ to hot spices（辛いスパイスに慣れていない味覚）

4.

_____ as a favored meal by the navy（人気の食事として海軍に採用される）

adopted　circulating　used　traders

Fact Checker

これは一般的な日本のカレーとインドのカレーを比較した表です。音声を聞いて、空所に当てはまる語を書き入れましょう。

	Japanese Curry	Indian Curry
Ingredients	Curry roux, vegetables, and ¹m_____ such as beef, chicken, or pork	A variety of ²s_____ and various meats, vegetables, or beans
Soup	Like a ³s_____	A ⁴w_____ curry sauce
Rice and others	Japonica rice	Indica rice or naan bread

 Try!

次の語句は日本のカレーとインドのカレーのどちらにより当てはまるか、分類しましょう。その後、ペアになって1〜4を交互に音読してみましょう。

1. mild   2. spicy   3. different spices   4. curry roux

Reading-Aloud Warm-Up

次の文は昭和初期に日本で人気を博したカレーについて書かれています。ペアになって1人ずつ音読し、相手の読み方と自分の読み方を比べてみましょう。

It's interesting to think that in the early Showa period, an Indian rebel against British rule escaped to Japan, married the daughter of a well-known bakery owner, and set up a curry house that became extremely popular.

Reading

本文を読んで、続く問題に取り組みましょう。

A If you were asked what meal is very popular in both British and Japanese homes, what would you say? A hamburger with French fries, maybe? Something with sausages? Actually, the answer is curry. As everyone knows, this is a dish with roots in ancient India. But a long time ago, it found a home in both Britain and Japan and has since become hugely popular.

B So what is curry? The name probably comes from the Tamil word "kari." In that language, it refers to a sauce made with spices and eaten with meat or vegetables. British traders in India heard the word and no doubt tried the food. They then took both the word and the food back home, and by the year 1750, curry recipes were already circulating in Britain. It was appreciated for its spicy flavor—so different from the duller flavors common in Britain at the time!—and became particularly popular in the Victorian era.

C The idea of curry found its way to Japan somewhat later, in the Meiji period. It was probably British traders who brought it, which is why it was seen as a Western dish. It was adapted to Japanese taste buds, which were not as used to hot spices as Indian tongues were, and the result was a dish that became uniquely Japanese. It was adopted as a favored meal by the Japanese army and navy, and that helped to spread the dish to all parts of the country. Even today, Japanese warships each have their own original recipe that is used on special occasions.

D It's interesting to think that in the early Showa period, an Indian rebel against British rule escaped to Japan, married the daughter of a well-known bakery owner, and set up a curry house that became extremely popular. His famous curry dish became known as "the taste of love and revolution." That dish—known in Japan today as *karee-raisu*—is now regarded by many in Japan as the country's favorite food!

Notes

Tamil「タミル語（インド南東部およびスリランカを中心に話される言葉）」　no doubt「間違いなく」
appreciate「高く評価する」　duller flavor「刺激のない味」　era「時代」　adapt to「改変する」
warship「軍艦」　rebel「反抗者」　set up「設立する」　revolution「革命」　regard「みなす」

Check!

本文のパラグラフ A ～ D の内容に合うように、正しい選択肢を選びましょう。

A 日本とイギリスの両方で人気の食事の代表格は [¹ ソーセージ / ² カレー / ³ ハンバーグ] である。

B イギリスにおけるカレーは、[¹ 貿易商によって伝えられた / ² ビクトリア朝時代後にもたらされた / ³ 従来よりまろやかな味が好まれた]。

C 日本のカレーは、[¹ 日本人用にアレンジが加えられた / ² 海上自衛隊が紹介した / ³ 明治時代よりも前にできあがっていた]。

D 「恋と革命のカレー」は、[¹ イギリス人と結婚したインド人 / ² 日本人と結婚したインド人 / ³ インド発祥のパン屋] によって生まれた。

Repeat and Look Up!

以下は本文中の2文です。日本語訳を完成させましょう。
次に教科書を閉じ、音声に続いてフレーズごとに声に出して暗唱しましょう。

1. It was adapted / to Japanese taste buds, / which were not as used to hot spices / as Indian tongues were. // （本文 l. 17）
   それは日本人の味覚に合うよう調整されました。日本人の味覚は、＿＿＿＿＿＿＿、
   ＿＿＿＿＿＿＿＿＿＿＿＿＿＿＿＿＿＿＿＿＿＿。

2. His famous curry dish became known / as "the taste of love and revolution." // （本文 l. 26）
   彼の有名なカレー料理は ＿＿＿＿＿＿＿＿＿＿＿＿＿＿＿＿＿＿＿＿。

Reading Aloud

「恋と革命のインドカレー」について書かれたパラグラフ D を、音読してみましょう。

1. まず太字で示された強く読む部分と 音読POINT の文に注意しながら、パラグラフ D の一部を聞きましょう。
   次に、自分でも ╱ と ‿ の記号（詳細は p.6）を書き込んでみましょう。

   DL 100　CD2-10

   音読POINT It's **in**teresting to **think** ╱ that in the **ear**ly **Sho**wa **per**iod, ╱ an **In**dian **re**bel against **Brit**ish **rule** ╱ [**es**caped to **Ja**pan,] ╱ [**mar**ried the **daugh**ter of a **well**-known **bak**ery **own**er,] ╱ and [**set** up a **cur**ry **house** that be**came** ex**treme**ly **pop**ular]. ╱╱ His **fa**mous **cur**ry **dish** be**came known** as "the **taste** of **love** and **rev**o**lu**tion." That **dish**—**known** in **Ja**pan to**day** as *karee-raisu*—is **now** re**gard**ed by **man**y in Ja**pan** as the **coun**try's **fa**vorite **food**!

   > **音読POINT 並列情報の読み方**
   >
   > ポイント文は、イギリス支配に対する反抗者のしたことを3つの動詞句で説明しています。Unit 1と同様に[　]のまとまりを意識することに加え、ここでは時系列で話が展開していることに注目しましょう。ストーリーの流れを遮らないように、AとBのまとまりの末尾はイントネーションを下げず、次のまとまりに向かって盛り上げるように読みましょう。

2. 最後に、ペアになって上の英文を1人ずつ音読し、*Check Points!* をもとに評価しあいましょう。

☑ *Check Points!*

❶ 強弱を意識し、リズムに乗って読めているか　　　　　　　　　　　　　　[　　／3点]
❷ 書き込んだ通りにポーズ、音のつながりを意識して読めているか　　　　　[　　／3点]
❸ ポイント文について、音読POINT を意識して読めているか　　　　　　　　[　　／3点]

Total Score: [　　／9点]

Retelling the Story

カレーがどのように日本に伝わったか、自分の言葉で再現してみましょう。

1. まずパラグラフ C の一部をもう一度聞き、下のイラストに関連するキーワードを書き込んでみましょう。

   DL 101   CD2-11

▶ Key Words

(   )

▶ Key Words

(   )

2. 次に、下の英文の下線部を補いながら、日本式カレーが生まれた背景を以下の3つの点に沿って紹介してみましょう。本文を見ずに、上のキーワードを参考にしたり、本文の表現を思い出したりしながら自分の言葉で話しましょう。

How Curry Found Its Way to Japan

| 時期 | Curry was introduced to Japan in _____.

| 伝えた人 | It was probably _____
_____.

| 日本式カレーの誕生 | It was adapted to _____
_____.

As a result, the dish _____.

Unit 10

Interacting with Others in a Globalized World

音読POINT 数字情報の読み方

Picture Dictionary

DL 102 CD2-12

日本語を参考に空所に入る語を選択肢から選び、イラストの説明を完成させましょう。

1.

More and more _____ visiting Japan（増え続ける訪日外国人）

2.

_____ up the suitcase without asking first（たずねることなくスーツケースを運ぶ）

3.

Never really be _____ into Japanese society（日本社会に受け入れられない）

4.

Be quite capable of using _____（きちんと箸を使うことができる）

```
pick   accepted   foreigners   chopsticks
```

Fact Checker

これは日本を旅行する外国の人々に向けた注意事項のリストです。音声を聞き、空所に当てはまる語を書き入れましょう。

Japan is friendly to travelers, but please remember these etiquette tips!
- Bowing: Bow ¹p_____ when you meet someone, thank them, or say goodbye.
- Shoes off: Remove shoes when ²e_____ a private home, traditional accommodation [*minshuku* or *ryokan*], or temple halls.
- Chopsticks: Remember that it is very ³i_____ to leave ⁴c_____ standing upright in a bowl of rice.

Try!

日本でのマナーについて書かれた以下の英文の空所に polite か impolite いずれかの単語を入れましょう。その後、ペアになって英文を1文ずつ音読してみましょう。

1. It is (　　　　　　) to bow to someone you meet for the first time.
2. It is (　　　　　　) to play with chopsticks when eating.

Reading-Aloud Warm-Up

次の文は訪日外国人観光客の増加について書かれたものです。ペアになって1人ずつ音読し、相手の読み方と自分の読み方を比べてみましょう。

The government hopes that by 2030, ten years after the second Tokyo Olympics, the number of tourists visiting Japan will reach 60 million a year, more than ten times the 2003 figure of 5.2 million.

Reading

本文を読んで、続く問題に取り組みましょう。

A It's no secret that more and more foreigners are visiting Japan. The government hopes that by 2030, ten years after the second Tokyo Olympics, the number of tourists visiting Japan will reach 60 million a year, more than ten times the 2003 figure of 5.2 million. In some ways, this is great for Japan. It means the country will benefit from tourists spending money, and it shows that people around the world are interested in Japan—its culture, its historical sites, its food, its beautiful landscapes.

B Fortunately for tourists, Japan is famed for its *omotenashi*—its hospitality—so visitors are sure to find a warm welcome. In hotels, in restaurants, on the Shinkansen, and in department stores, visitors to Japan are treated better than they would be in any other country. As the *Wall Street Journal* once put it, "Japan has perfected hospitality culture."

C However, although the Japanese can rightly take pride in their hospitality culture, they have not been immune to criticism from outsiders. For instance, some foreigners feel that service in Japan can sometimes become excessive, such as when a hotel bellhop automatically picks up a guest's suitcase without asking first. Others have argued that although visitors are treated very politely, that stops them from feeling at home. They get a sense that they could never really be accepted into Japanese society.

D Some tourists have written about their experiences and their feelings online. In one example, a woman complained about being given a spoon and a fork when she bought a Japanese-style *bento* at a convenience store. She was quite capable of using chopsticks, but the young man behind the counter assumed she couldn't, so he gave her a spoon and a fork. He was trying to be helpful, but the woman felt he should not make assumptions like that.

E It's good that Japanese service tries to be helpful and polite. But it's also important to understand what a visitor truly wants while in Japan. That is the best way to make tourists feel the true warmth and friendliness of the people of Japan.

30

Notes

benefit「利益を得る」 landscape「風景」 famed for「〜で名高い」 perfect「完成させる」
immune「影響を受けていない」 excessive「過剰な」 bellhop「荷物係、ベルボーイ」 complain「不満を言う」
assume「予想する」

Check!

本文のパラグラフ A 〜 D の内容に合うように、正しい選択肢を選びましょう。

A 訪日外国人観光客の増加は、[¹ 日本の科学技術 / ² 日本文化 / ³ 移民政策] への興味の高まりを示している。

B 日本のおもてなし文化は、[¹ ホテルから始まった / ² 他の国にも影響を与えている / ³ 海外メディアでも報じられた]。

C 日本のおもてなし文化は、[¹ 批判されることもある / ² 常にくつろぎを与える / ³ 一流ホテルで体験するとよい]。

D ある外国人女性は [¹ 客に横柄に接する / ² 誤った先入観で接客をする / ³ 外国語を話せない] コンビニ店員とのやりとりについて、インターネット上に綴った。

Repeat and Look Up!

DL 109, 110　CD2-19　CD2-20

以下の2文は本文中の英文です。日本語訳を完成させましょう。
次に教科書を閉じ、音声に続いてフレーズごとに声に出して暗唱しましょう。

1. It means / the country will benefit from tourists / spending money. //
（本文 l. 5）
それは _____ ことを意味します。

2. The hotel bellhop / automatically picks up a guest's suitcase / without asking first. // （本文 l. 16、一部改変）
そのホテルの荷物係は、お客さんのスーツケースを _____ 。

Reading Aloud

訪日外国人観光客数の政府目標について書かれたパラグラフ A を音読してみましょう。

1. まず太字で示された強く読む部分と 音読POINT の文に注意しながら、パラグラフ A の一部を聞きましょう。
   次に、自分でも / と ⌣ の記号 (詳細は p.6) を書き込んでみましょう。

   🎧 DL 111　💿 CD2-21

It's **no se**cret that **more** and **more for**eigners are **vis**iting Ja**pan**. 音読POINT The **gov**ernment **hopes** / that [① by **2030**, / **ten years** after the **sec**ond **To**kyo O**lym**pics], / the **num**ber of **tour**ists **vis**iting Japan / will ② **reach 60 mil**lion a **year**, / **more** than **ten times** / [the **2003 fig**ure of **5.2 mil**lion]. // In **some** ways, this is **great** for Ja**pan**. It **means** the **coun**try will **ben**efit from **tour**ists **spend**ing **mon**ey.

音読POINT 数字情報をはっきりと伝える

ポイント文には数字情報が複数含まれます。2つの山を意識しましょう。最初の山「2030年＝東京オリンピックの10年後」という情報は、1つのまとまりを意識します。そして2つ目の山「6,000万人に到達」の部分に頂点が来るよう、will reach の後で軽く息継ぎをして、60 million をはっきり発音しましょう。

---

2. 最後に、ペアになって上の英文を1人ずつ音読し、*Check Points!* をもとに評価しあいましょう。

✓ *Check Points!*

❶ 強弱を意識し、リズムに乗って読めているか　　　　　　　　　　　　　[　　/ 3点]
❷ 書き込んだ通りにポーズ、音のつながりを意識して読めているか　　　　[　　/ 3点]
❸ ポイント文について、音読POINT を意識して読めているか　　　　　　　[　　/ 3点]

Total Score: [　　/ 9点]

Retelling the Story

外国人からみた日本のサービスについて、自分の言葉で再現してみましょう。

1. まずパラグラフ C をもう一度聞き、下のイラストに関連するキーワードを書き込んでみましょう。

　　　　　　　　　　　　　　　　　　　　　　　　🎧 DL 112　💿 CD2-22

▶ Key Words　　　　　　　　　　　　　　▶ Key Words

(　　　　　　　　　　　　)　　　　(　　　　　　　　　　　　)

2. 次に、下の英文の下線部を補いながら、日本のサービスについて不満を抱いた経験のある外国人からの意見を2つ、紹介してみましょう。本文を見ずに、上のキーワードを参考にしたり、本文の表現を思い出したりしながら自分の言葉で話しましょう。

Foreigners' Views on Japanese Hospitality

Although the Japanese are famed for their hospitality culture, there are some criticisms of it.

意見1 Some foreigners feel _____.

There are times, for example, when a hotel bellhop _____
_____.

意見2 Others have argued that although visitors are treated politely, _____
_____.

They get a sense that _____.

Unit 11

The Tragedy of Rana Plaza

音読POINT 核心から詳細を述べる

Picture Dictionary

DL 113　CD2-23

日本語を参考にして空所に入る語を選択肢から選び、イラストの説明を完成させましょう。

1.

Workers in _____ making cheap clothes（安い服を作る工場の労働者）

2.

The worst clothing-factory _____ in history
（史上最悪の服飾工場での事故）

3.

High-quality clothes made by _____（手仕事で作られる高品質の衣類）

4.

Women who take _____ in their work（仕事に誇りを持つ女性たち）

factories　hand　pride　accident

Fact Checker

🎧 DL 114 💿 CD2-24

これはイギリスのテレグラフ紙で紹介された、女優のエマ・ワトソンがバングラデシュの縫製工場を訪れた時の言葉です。音声を聞き、空所に当てはまる語を書き入れましょう。

"The ¹f_____ world can be savage and ²c_____. (…) When I went to Bangladesh, to a ³f_____ where clothes are made, it was horrifying. There is a ⁴c_____ to cheap clothes—if people could see the inhumane way they're made, they would never in a million years buy them…"

Adapted from *The Telegraph*, July 01, 2011

Notes savage「残忍な」 inhumane「非人道的な」

 Try!

次の各単語のもっとも強く発音される部分に印をつけましょう。その後、ペアになって1〜4を交互に音読しましょう。

1. savage　　**2.** cruel　　**3.** Bangladesh　　**4.** horrifying

Reading-Aloud Warm-Up

次の文はある建物の崩落事故の原因について書かれたものです。ペアになって1人ずつ音読し、相手の読み方と自分の読み方を比べてみましょう。

Why did the building collapse? The root of the problem was greed in the fashion industry—the desire to make as much money as possible.

Reading

本文を読んで、続く問題に取り組みましょう。

A "The fashion world can be savage and cruel." These are the words of the British actress Emma Watson. She was talking about the tough life of a fashion model, but also about the terrible conditions for workers in factories making cheap clothes. The truth of her words became especially clear after the collapse of the Rana Plaza building, in Bangladesh, in 2013.

B The Rana Plaza contained shops, apartments, and factories making clothes for well-known brands like Gap, UNIQLO, and Zara. It was a huge building, with thousands of men and women working in the factories for very low wages. On April 24, 2013, the building collapsed. Over a thousand people lost their lives. It was the worst clothing-factory accident in history.

C Why did the building collapse? The root of the problem was greed in the fashion industry—the desire to make as much money as possible. The builders used cheap construction materials. They also added extra unapproved floors and heavy machinery to produce large quantities of clothing cheaply. When we look back now, it is no surprise that such a terrible accident occurred.

D However, other places in Bangladesh's clothing industry give us reason for hope. On the western border of the country, there is a small village called Thanapara. An organization called the Thanapara Swallows has helped the women of the village develop the skills needed—dyeing cotton thread, weaving it into cloth, and sewing the pieces together. Nearly everything is done by hand, but they still make the highest-quality clothing. Their minimum wage, about 50 euros, is low compared with our standards, but the most skilled can earn more than twice that. Above all, the women working there take great pride in their work.

E As a result of their work, consumers everywhere can buy beautiful and comfortable clothing at very reasonable prices. This is good for us as consumers, but we should always take into account the conditions under which our clothing has been made. Doing that makes a fitting memorial to the victims of the Rana Plaza tragedy, showing that the fashion world doesn't need to be savage and cruel to succeed.

Notes

wage「賃金」 root「根本」 greed「欲深さ」 construction material「建設資材」
unapproved「認められていない」 machinery「機械類」 dye「染める」 weave「編む」 sew「縫う」
reasonable prices「手頃な値段」 take into account「考慮に入れる」 fitting「適した」

Check!

本文のパラグラフ B ～ E の内容に合うように、正しい選択肢を選びましょう。

B ラナプラザ・ビルでは、[¹ 多くの女性と子ども / ² 約1,000人の縫製工場スタッフ / ³ 何千人もの低賃金労働者] が働いていた。

C 建物崩落の原因は [¹ 利益を追求する欲深さ / ² 未だに調査中 / ³ テロリストによる陰謀] である。

D バングラデシュ西端の村では、[¹ ラナプラザと同様の事故が起こった / ² 衣料品の品質向上が課題である / ³ 労働者の技術向上を支援する組織がある]。

E 私たちのすべきことは [¹ 作り手の労働環境への配慮 / ² ファッション業界への制裁 / ³ できるだけ高価な洋服を買うこと] である。

Repeat and Look Up!

以下は本文中の2文です。日本語訳を完成させましょう。
次に教科書を閉じ、音声に続いてフレーズごとに声に出して暗唱しましょう。

1. When we look back now, / it is no surprise / that such a terrible accident occurred. //（本文 l. 15）
今になって振り返ると、_____
_____。

2. Nearly everything is done by hand, / but they still make / the highest-quality clothing. //（本文 l. 21）
_____が、それでも彼らは最高品質の衣類を作っています。

Reading Aloud

ラナプラザ崩落事故の原因を説明したパラグラフ C を音読してみましょう。

1. まず太字で示された強く読む部分と 音読POINT の文に注意しながら、パラグラフ C を聞きましょう。
   次に、自分でも / と ⌣ の記号（詳細はp.6）を書き込んでみましょう。

   DL 122　CD2-32

Why did the **build**ing col**lapse**? 音読POINT The **root** of the **prob**lem / was **greed** in the **fash**ion in**dus**try / — the de**sire** to **make** as **much mon**ey as **pos**sible. // The **build**ers **used cheap** con**struc**tion materials. // They **also add**ed **ex**tra unap**proved floors** and **heav**y ma**chin**ery to pro**duce large quan**tities of **cloth**ing **cheap**ly. When we **look back now**, it is **no** sur**prise** that such a **ter**rible **ac**cident oc**cur**red.

音読POINT 核心から詳細を述べる

ポイント文では悲劇的な事故の原因が、核心→詳細に移る手法で語られています。1文目のgreed in the fashion industry は強い意味を持つ言葉なので、ゆっくり、はっきり読みましょう。ダッシュの前や1文目の後には十分にポーズを取り、余韻を残すことも大切です。そうすることで、make as much money as...や2文目の The builders used...という事故に関する詳細情報を、聞き手はより理解しやすくなります。

---

2. 最後に、ペアになって上の英文を1人ずつ音読し、*Check Points!* をもとに評価しあいましょう。

☑ *Check Points!*

❶ 強弱を意識し、リズムに乗って読めているか　　　　　　　　　　　　　　　[　/3点]
❷ 書き込んだ通りにポーズ、音のつながりを意識して読めているか　　　　　　[　/3点]
❸ ポイント文について、音読POINT を意識して読めているか　　　　　　　　　[　/3点]

Total Score:　/9点

Retelling the Story

バングラデシュ西部にあるタナパラ・スワローズについて、自分の言葉で再現してみましょう。

1. まずパラグラフ D をもう一度聞き、下のイラストに関連するキーワードを書き込んでみましょう。

   DL 123　CD2-33

▶ Key Words

(　　　　　　　　　　　　)　(　　　　　　　　　　　　)

▶ Key Words

2. 次に、下の英文の下線部を補いながら、タナパラ・スワローズの製品とそこで働く女性たちについて紹介してみましょう。本文を見ずに、上のキーワードを参考にしたり、本文の表現を思い出したりしながら自分の言葉で話しましょう。

Hope in Bangladesh's Clothing Industry

On the western border of the country, there is an organization called the

_____.

製品について The women in the village have the skills of _____

_____.

Nearly everything is _____.

働く女性たちについて Their minimum wage is not high, but the women

working there _____.

Unit 12

The Age of Innocence

音読POINT 感情を込めて読む

Picture Dictionary

DL 124　CD2-34

日本語を参考にして空所に入る語を選択肢から選び、イラストの説明を完成させましょう。

1.

An old man with a big white _____（大きな白いあごひげのあるおじいさん）

2.

Write to a newspaper to ask if Santa _____（新聞に投書してサンタの存在を尋ねる）

3.

_____ gifts under the Christmas tree（クリスマスツリーの下にギフトを置く）

4.

An older brother who already knows the _____（すでに真実を知っている兄）

truth　exists　beard　put

Fact Checker

以下は、今から100年以上も前の1897年に、アメリカに住む少女バージニア（当時8歳）がニューヨークの新聞に投書した手紙です。音声を聞き、空所に当てはまる語を書き入れましょう。

Dear Editor:
I am 8 years old.
Some of my little friends say ¹t_____ ²i_____ no Santa Claus.
Papa says, "If you see it in The Sun, it's so."
Please ³t_____ me the ⁴t_____: Is there a Santa Claus?

VIRGINIA O'HANLON
115 WEST NINETY-FIFTH STREET

Note The Sun「サン紙」（かつてニューヨークで発行されていた新聞）

 Try!

上の Is there a Santa Claus? という疑問に対し、以下の２つの答えが寄せられました。空所に適切な英文を選択肢から選びましょう。その後、ペアになって質問と応答の会話をしてみましょう。

1. No, there is no such man. _____
2. Yes, there is a Santa Claus. _____

> **a.** It is impossible for a man to deliver presents to all the children on earth.
> **b.** He does indeed exist, but in a special way.

Reading-Aloud Warm-Up

次の文では、サンタクロースの存在を子どもに語りかけています。ペアになって１人ずつ音読し、相手の読み方と自分の読み方を比べてみましょう。

There is a Santa Claus. He exists as certainly as love and generosity and devotion exist. Alas! How dreary would be the world if there were no Santa Claus!

Reading

本文を読んで、続く問題に取り組みましょう。

A Did you believe in Santa Claus when you were a child? For many people, a belief in Santa Claus is part of the magic of childhood. The secret—that he exists only in our imagination—is something many parents work hard to keep. Eventually, of course, children discover that their presents come from Mom and Dad, not from a kind old man with a red suit and a big white beard. Excited children, unable to sleep on Christmas Eve, may see their parents putting presents under the Christmas tree. Some are told by an older brother or sister who already knows the truth. Others just realize by themselves that one man couldn't possibly deliver presents to all the children on earth in a single night!

B Can you remember the time when you realized that there was no Santa Claus? Were you upset? Maybe so, but it's a good opportunity for parents to teach children something important—that having a sense of wonder about the world is something to value.

C Perhaps the most famous example of this came over a hundred years ago. A little girl called Virginia wrote to an American newspaper to ask if Santa existed. The paper's editor answered her difficult question in a wonderfully warm way. He said that while it was true that nobody can see Santa Claus, that doesn't mean that Santa Claus does not exist. He does indeed exist, but in a special way. Here is part of the editor's response:

"Yes, Virginia, there is a Santa Claus. He exists as certainly as love and generosity and devotion exist. (…) Alas! How dreary would be the world if there were no Santa Claus! It would be as dreary as if there were no Virginias."

D This warm and gentle response showed that we should believe in good things. Even if they are only in our imagination, good things help to make life worth living. So if a child asks you tomorrow whether Santa Claus exists or not, what will you say?

Notes

realize 認識する　possibly 「(否定文で) とても〜ない」　opportunity 「機会」
a sense of wonder 「不思議に思う気持ち、好奇心」　editor 「編集者」　wonderfully 「すばらしく」
generosity 「寛大さ」　devotion 「献身、信心」　dreary 「わびしい、退屈な」

Check!

本文のパラグラフ A 〜 D の内容に合うように、正しい選択肢を選びましょう。

A 多くの親は、サンタクロースの存在を子どもに [¹ 隠そうとする / ² 信じさせようとする / ³ 説明する]。

B 世の中について [¹ 懐疑的な / ² 不思議に思う / ³ 解明する] 気持ちを持つことを教えるのは大切である。

C ある新聞の編集者は、サンタクロースは [¹ よい子にだけ見える / ² 見えないけれど存在する / ³ 見えないので存在しない] と語った。

D 編集者の答えは、よいことを [¹ 信じる / ² 他人に伝える / ³ 具体化する] ことの大切さを示している。

Repeat and Look Up!

🎧 DL 130, 131　　💿 CD2-40　　💿 CD2-41

以下は本文中の2文です。日本語訳を完成させましょう。
次に教科書を閉じ、音声に続いてフレーズごとに声に出して暗唱しましょう。

1. Others just realize by themselves / that one man couldn't possibly deliver presents / to all the children on earth / in a single night! //　（本文 l. 8）
   他の子どもたちは、一人の男の人が＿＿。

2. While it is true / that nobody can see Santa Claus, / that doesn't mean / that Santa Claus does not exist. //　（本文 l. 18、一部改変）
   ＿＿＿＿＿＿＿＿＿＿＿＿＿＿＿＿＿＿＿＿＿＿＿＿＿＿は真実である一方で、それは＿＿＿＿＿＿＿＿＿＿＿＿＿＿＿＿＿＿＿＿＿＿ということを意味するわけではありません。

Reading Aloud

「サンタはいるの?」という疑問に答えた社説についてのパラグラフ C を、音読してみましょう。

1. まず太字で示された強く読む部分と 音読POINT の文に注意しながら、パラグラフ C の一部を聞きましょう。
   次に、自分でも / と ⌣ の記号（詳細は p.6）を書き込んでみましょう。

   🎧 DL 132   💿 CD2-42

He **said** that while it was **true** that **no**body can **see San**ta **Claus**, that **doesn't mean** that **San**ta **Claus** does not ex**ist**. He **does** in**deed** ex**ist**, but in a **spec**ial **way**. Here is **part** of the **ed**itor's re**sponse**:

音読POINT "**Yes**, **Virgin**ia, / there **is** a **San**ta **Claus**. // He ex**ists** / as **cer**tainly as **love** and gene**ros**ity and de**vot**ion / ex**ist**. // (…) **Alas**! // **How drear**y would be the **world** / if there were **no San**ta **Claus**! // It would be as **drear**y as if there were **no Virgin**ias."

音読POINT 感情を込めて読む

ポイント文の前半は、「サンタが存在する」という内容を現在形の there is と exists を使って述べています。現在形は「不変の真実」を表すため、きっぱりと言い切るように読むとよいでしょう。Alas! 以降は情熱的に読みます。How dreary...の文は「もしサンタがいなかったら」と残念な気持ちを想像し、イントネーションも高めにして読んでみましょう。

---

2. 最後に、ペアになって上の英文を1人ずつ音読し、**Check Points!** をもとに評価しあいましょう。

☑ ***Check Points!***
❶ 強弱を意識し、リズムに乗って読めているか　　　　　　　　　　　[　/3点]
❷ 書き込んだ通りにポーズ、音のつながりを意識して読めているか　　[　/3点]
❸ ポイント文について、音読POINT を意識して読めているか　　　　　[　/3点]

Total Score: [　/9点]

Retelling the Story

子どもがサンタクロースの正体を知るきっかけについて、自分の言葉で再現してみましょう。

1. まずパラグラフ A の一部をもう一度聞き、下のイラストに関連するキーワードを書き込んでみましょう。

▶ Key Words

(   )

▶ Key Words

(   )

2. 次に、下の英文の下線部を補いながら、サンタクロースの正体を知る3つのありそうなきっかけについて紹介してみましょう。本文を見ずに、上のキーワードを参考にしたり、本文の表現を思い出したりしながら自分の言葉で話しましょう。

How Children Come to Realize There Is No Santa Claus

Children come to realize that there is no Santa Claus in different ways.

きっかけ① Excited children, unable to sleep on Christmas Eve, ＿＿＿＿＿

＿＿＿＿＿＿＿＿＿＿＿＿＿＿＿＿＿＿＿＿＿＿＿＿＿＿＿＿＿＿＿＿＿＿＿.

きっかけ② Some are told ＿＿＿＿＿＿＿＿＿＿＿＿＿＿＿＿＿＿＿＿＿＿

＿＿＿＿＿＿＿＿＿＿＿＿＿＿＿＿＿＿＿＿＿＿＿＿＿＿＿＿＿＿＿＿＿＿＿.

きっかけ③ Others just realize that one man couldn't possibly deliver ＿＿

＿＿＿＿＿＿＿＿＿＿＿＿＿＿＿＿＿＿＿＿＿＿＿＿＿＿＿＿＿＿＿＿＿＿＿.

Unit 13

Kiribati: A Paradise on Earth— But for How Much Longer?

音読POINT 他の人の発言を紹介する

DL 134　CD2-44

Picture Dictionary

日本語を参考にして空所に入る語を選択肢から選び、イラストの説明を完成させましょう。

1.

A powerful _____ with the ocean（海との強い結びつき）

2.

Storms that bring high _____（高潮をもたらす嵐）

3.

_____ such as breadfruit, bananas, and bwabwai
（パンノキの実、バナナ、パパイなどの作物）

4.

Mangroves to _____ down erosion（浸食を抑制するマングローブ）

| bond　crops　slow　tides |

Fact Checker

これは地球温暖化によって海面上昇が起こる理由を説明したイラストと説明文です。
音声を聞き、空所に当てはまる語を書き入れましょう。

Sea-Level Rise—Why Is It Happening?

❶ Seawater Expansion

When water ¹h_____ up, it expands. Warmer oceans occupy more space, causing a ²r_____ in the sea level.

❷ Melting Glaciers

Glaciers naturally melt a bit each summer, but higher temperatures caused by ³g_____ warming result in more summer ⁴m_____.

Try!

次の地球温暖化に関連する言葉を完成させましょう。その後、ペアになって1〜3を交互に音読しましょう。

1. 地球温暖化　（　　　　　）（　　　　　　）
2. 海面上昇　　sea-(　　　　　) (　　　　　　)
3. 気温上昇　　higher (　　　　　　)

Reading-Aloud Warm Up

次の文では、水没の危機に直面する人たちの言葉が紹介されています。ペアになって1人ずつ音読し、相手の読み方と自分の読み方を比べてみましょう。

One young mother says, "Kiribati is the best place for my sons, regardless of the threats." Another declares, "We will not be victims—we will not be a defeated people!"

Reading

本文を読んで、続く問題に取り組みましょう。

A Kiribati is a tiny nation of many islands in the middle of the vast Pacific Ocean. It has been the home of the I-Kiribati people since ancient times. But the islands of Kiribati are very flat—no hills or mountains—and as sea levels slowly rise around the world, these islands are gradually disappearing under water.

B Over the centuries, the I-Kiribati have established a powerful bond with the ocean. They are experts at fishing, and have long understood the moods of the water as it changed throughout the year. They even catch food on the beaches, collecting cockles and sea snails to cook in a coconut shell over a smoky fire.

C But now, as the world's climate begins to change, the ocean is no longer so friendly. Storms bring high tides, eating away at their coastline, washing over their land, and bringing salt to the water they drink. This salt affects not just their drinking water, but the water they use for their crops, too. These include breadfruit, bananas, and the all-important bwabwai, which is central to Kiribati culture, eaten at all the major feasts. It may well disappear completely from Kiribati.

D As a result of these changes, some of the younger generation are moving away to build a future elsewhere. But others are staying, determined to adapt and live on in the land they love. One young mother says, "Kiribati is the best place for my sons, regardless of the threats." Another declares, "We will not be victims—we will not be a defeated people!" Positive action is being taken by the islanders: building sea walls and planting mangroves to slow down erosion; collecting more rainwater for drinking water; and using modern technology like solar power.

E The people of Kiribati are proud of their beautiful islands and refuse to abandon them because of changes in the climate. Their great spirit and commitment to their land and way of life will surely be tested in the years to come. But they are determined to win in the end.

Notes

cockle「サルガイ（食用になる２枚貝）」 sea snail「巻貝」 shell「殻」 eat away「侵食する」
breadfruit「パンノキの実」 bwaibwai「パパイ（タロイモの一種で、英訳は giant swamp taro。栽培に時間がかかるため貴重な作物とされ、結婚式や大きなセレモニーの際に提供される）」 feast「宴会、祝いごと」
adapt「適応する」 regardless of「～に関係なく」 victim「犠牲者」 defeat「負かす」 erosion「侵食」
commitment「献身」

Check!

本文のパラグラフ A ～ D の内容に合うように、正しい選択肢を選びましょう。

A キリバス共和国は [¹ かつて海底都市だった / ² 山と海が豊富である / ³ 海に沈みつつある]。

B 島の人々は [¹ 海と共存してきた / ² 海と戦ってきた / ³ 海を支配してきた]。

C 気候変動により、[¹ 栽培用水に影響が出ている / ² 宴会の是非が疑問視されている / ³ 塩湖ができた]。

D 海面上昇への対抗策の１つとして、[¹ マングローブの伐採 / ² 若い技術者の育成 / ³ 雨水の有効活用] があげられる。

Repeat and Look Up!

DL 141, 142　　CD2-51　　CD2-52

以下は本文中の２文です。日本語訳を完成させましょう。
次に教科書を閉じ、音声に続いてフレーズごとに声に出して暗唱しましょう。

1. This salt affects / not just their drinking water, / but the water they use for their crops, too. // （本文 l. 13）
   塩害は ＿＿＿＿＿＿＿＿＿＿＿＿＿＿＿＿＿＿＿＿ だけでなく、＿＿＿＿＿＿
   ＿＿＿＿＿＿＿＿＿＿＿＿＿＿＿。

2. As a result of these changes, / some of the younger generation are moving away / to build a future elsewhere. // （本文 l. 18）
   これらの変化の結果、若い世代の人の中には ＿＿＿＿＿＿＿＿＿＿
   ＿＿＿＿＿＿＿＿＿＿＿＿＿。

Reading Aloud

水没に対するキリバスの人々の反応について書かれたパラグラフ D を音読してみましょう。

1. まず太字で示された強く読む部分と 音読POINT の文に注意しながら、パラグラフ D の一部を聞きましょう。
   次に、自分でも / と ⌣ の記号（詳細は p.6）を書き込んでみましょう。

   DL 143　CD2-53

As a re**sult** of these **changes**, some of the **young**er gener**a**tion are **mov**ing a**way** to **build** a **fu**ture **else**where. But **oth**ers are **stay**ing, de**ter**mined to a**dapt** and **live on** in the **land** they **love**. 音読POINT **One young mot**her **says**, / "**Kiribati** is the **best place** for my **sons**, / re**gard**less of the **threats**." // **Anoth**er de**clares**, / "We **will not** be **vict**ims / —we **will not** be a de**feat**ed **peo**ple!" //

音読POINT 他の人の発言を紹介する

ポイント文にはキリバスの人々の実際の発言が含まれています。引用部分に入る前に一呼吸置き、人々の気持ちを想像しながら読みましょう。逆に引用以外の部分は淡々と読むことで差をつけるとよいでしょう。"We will not be victims..." の文は特に強い意志を感じさせる発言です。will not の will は助動詞で機能語ですが、このように強い意味を持つ場合は will not をまるごと強調して読みましょう。

---

2. 最後に、ペアになって上の英文を1人ずつ音読し、***Check Points!*** をもとに評価しあいましょう。

✓ *Check Points!*
❶ 強弱を意識し、リズムに乗って読めているか　　　　　　　　　　　　[　　/3点]
❷ 書き込んだ通りにポーズ、音のつながりを意識して読めているか　　　[　　/3点]
❸ ポイント文について、音読POINT を意識して読めているか　　　　　　[　　/3点]

Total Score:　[　　/9点]

Retelling the Story

キリバスにおける海面上昇の脅威について、自分の言葉で再現してみましょう。

1. まずパラグラフ C をもう一度聞き、下のイラストに関連するキーワードを書き込んでみましょう。

   🎧 DL 144　💿 CD2-54

▶ Key Words　　　　　　　　　　　▶ Key Words

(　　　　　　　　　　　　　)　　(　　　　　　　　　　　　　)

2. 次に、下の英文の下線部を補いながら、海面上昇がキリバスに及ぼす２つの脅威を紹介してみましょう。本文を見ずに、上のキーワードを参考にしたり、本文の表現を思い出したりしながら自分の言葉で話しましょう。

How the Ocean Threatens the Kiribati Way of Life

The ocean is no longer so friendly to the people of Kiribati.

脅威1　Storms bring ＿＿＿＿＿＿＿, eating away ＿＿＿＿＿＿＿＿＿＿,

washing over ＿＿＿＿＿＿, and bringing ＿＿＿＿＿＿＿＿＿＿＿.

脅威2　Salt affects ＿＿＿＿＿＿＿＿＿＿＿＿＿＿＿＿＿＿＿＿＿

＿＿＿＿＿＿＿＿＿＿＿＿＿＿＿＿＿＿＿＿＿＿＿＿＿＿＿＿＿＿.

The bwabwai may well ＿＿＿＿＿＿＿＿＿＿＿＿＿＿＿＿＿＿.

Unit 14

Two Great Painters...and a Stormy Friendship

音読POINT メッセージの中心を際立たせる

Picture Dictionary

DL 145　CD2-55

日本語を参考に空所に入る語を選択肢から選び、イラストの説明を完成させましょう。

1.

Live a life of _____
（貧困の生活を送る）

2.

New _____ and light in Arles（アルルでの新しい景色と光）

3.

_____ the guest's room with paintings（客間を絵で明るくする）

4.

Two artists who began to _____
（ケンカを始めた2人の芸術家）

---

brighten　poverty　landscapes　quarrel

Fact Checker

以下は、東京・新宿にある東郷青児記念 損保ジャパン日本興亜美術館が所有するゴッホの絵画『ひまわり』の説明です。音声を聞き、空所に当てはまる語を書き入れましょう。

Van Gogh produced twelve "sunflower" paintings. He painted seven of them during his stay in Arles, ¹F_____.

This is one of them. He ²w_____ to ³d_____ one of the rooms in his house for his ⁴f_____ artist, Paul Gauguin.

Sunflowers, 1888
Oil on canvas

Try!

次の固有名詞の英語での読み方を確認し、日本語での呼び方との違いを理解しましょう。その後、ペアになって1～3を交互に音読しましょう。

1. van Gogh　　2. Arles　　3. Paul Gauguin

Reading-Aloud Warm-Up

次の文はひまわりという花の名前がもつ意味について書かれたものです。ペアになって1人ずつ音読し、相手の読み方と自分の読み方を比べてみましょう。

Sunflowers are called that because of the large, round, yellow flowers the plant produces. They are often regarded as symbols of friendship and faithfulness.

Reading

本文を読んで、続く問題に取り組みましょう。

A In a museum of art in Tokyo you will find one of the world's most famous flower paintings: Vincent van Gogh's "Sunflowers." It shows fifteen large sunflowers arranged in a yellow vase. The Dutch painter produced this beautiful work in 1888, but behind this bright painting there is a rather dark story.

B As a young artist, van Gogh had little success selling his work, and he lived a life of poverty. When his health began to decline, he decided to move to Arles, a city in the south of France.

C There, van Gogh found something that changed his approach to painting: new landscapes and a quality of light he had not seen before. He began to produce pictures with brighter, more vibrant colors.

D One day, he came up with the idea of inviting a friend and fellow artist to live with him in Arles. The friend's name was Paul Gauguin. Gauguin agreed, and van Gogh decided to brighten his guest's room with some sunflower paintings.

E Sunflowers are called that because of the large, round, yellow flowers the plant produces. They are often regarded as symbols of friendship and faithfulness, which is why van Gogh chose them for Gauguin. He made artistic use of colors and brush strokes to create paintings with a powerful effect on the viewer.

F Unfortunately, the two artists soon began to quarrel. There was a famous incident when van Gogh, in a mental breakdown after an argument, cut off his own ear with a razor. Gauguin was shocked by this behavior and decided to return to Paris.

G Despite their disagreements, the two artists influenced one another considerably. Interestingly, Gauguin admired the sunflower paintings, a feeling that grew stronger after he heard of van Gogh's death.

H Of course, we do not know exactly what the paintings meant to Gauguin: the meaning of a painting varies from person to person. But for many people, the sunflower series represents life, loyalty, and friendship. Find an example of van Gogh's sunflower series and have a good look at it. What does the picture say to you?

Notes

decline「悪化する」 vibrant「活気に満ちた」 fellow「仲間」 faithfulness「忠誠」 brush stroke「筆使い」
mental breakdown「神経衰弱」 argument「口論」 considerably「かなり」 loyalty「忠誠」

Check!

本文のパラグラフ B C D F G の内容に合うように、正しい選択肢を選びましょう。

B　ゴッホは若い頃に [¹ 作品が売れず / ² 常に健康状態が悪く / ³ アルルという町が肌に合わず] 苦労した。

C D　アルルにてゴッホは、[¹ 自身の寝室にひまわりの絵を飾った / ² ゴーギャンに出会った / ³ 新しい表現法を使い始めた]。

F　ゴッホはゴーギャンとのケンカの後、[¹ ゴーギャンの耳を切った / ² 自身の耳を切った / ³ ゴーギャンを家から追い出した]。

G　ゴーギャンはゴッホと別れた後、[¹ ゴッホを恨んでいた / ² ゴッホの作品をたたえた / ³ ケンカしたことを後悔した]。

Repeat and Look Up!

DL 155, 156　CD2-65　CD2-66

以下は本文中の2文です。日本語訳を完成させましょう。
次に教科書を閉じ、音声に続いてフレーズごとに声に出して暗唱しましょう。

1. Van Gogh decided to brighten his guest's room / with some sunflower paintings. // (本文 l. 14)
   ヴァン・ゴッホは＿＿＿＿＿＿＿＿＿＿＿＿＿＿＿＿＿＿＿＿＿を決めました。

2. They are often regarded / as symbols of friendship and faithfulness, / which is why van Gogh chose them / for Gauguin. // (本文 l. 17)
   それらはしばしば友情と忠誠の象徴とみなされますが、＿＿＿＿＿＿＿＿＿
   ＿＿＿＿＿＿＿＿＿＿＿＿＿＿＿＿＿＿＿＿＿＿＿＿＿＿＿＿＿＿＿。

Reading Aloud

ゴッホ作『ひまわり』の背景にあるメッセージについて書かれたパラグラフ E を音読してみましょう。

1. まず太字で示された強く読む部分と 音読POINT の文に注意しながら、パラグラフ E の一部を聞きましょう。
   次に、自分でも / と ⌣ の記号（詳細は p.6）を書き込んでみましょう。

   DL 157   CD2-67

音読POINT **Sun**flowers are **called** that / because of the **large, round, yel**low **flow**ers / [the **plant** pro**duc**es]. // They are **of**ten re**gard**ed as **sym**bols of **friend**ship and **faith**fulness, / which is why **van Gogh chose** them / for Gau**guin**. // He made ar**tis**tic **use** of **col**ors and **brush strokes** to cre**ate paint**ings with a **pow**erful ef**fect** on the **view**er.

音読POINT　メッセージの中心を際立たせる

語単位だけでなく、句や節の単位でも強弱を考えて読む必要があります。英語では、すでに述べられたことと関連する内容（旧情報）を文の前半に、新しい情報を含む内容（新情報）を後半に置くことが多く、ポイント文の1文目はその一例です。新情報を際立たせるため、because of the large, round, yellow flowers の句をその前の部分よりも強調して読みましょう。一方、2文目では後半の which is why 以下は補足情報です。そのため、前半部、中でもメッセージの中心となる friendship and faithfulness を際立たせて読みます。

---

2. 最後に、ペアになって上の英文を1人ずつ音読し、*Check Points!* をもとに評価しあいましょう。

✓ *Check Points!*
① 強弱を意識し、リズムに乗って読めているか　　　　　　　　　　　　　　[　　/3点]
② 書き込んだ通りにポーズ、音のつながりを意識して読めているか　　　　　[　　/3点]
③ ポイント文について、音読POINT を意識して読めているか　　　　　　　　[　　/3点]

Total Score: 　/9点

Retelling the Story

ゴッホがアルルに移住してからの生活について、自分の言葉で再現してみましょう。

1. まずパラグラフ B ～ D をもう一度聞き、下のイラストに関連するキーワードを書き込んでみましょう。

 DL 158   CD2-68

▶ Key Words   ▶ Key Words

(   )   (   )

2. 次に、下の英文の下線部を補いながら、ゴッホのアルル移住後の主な変化について、以下の2つの点に沿って紹介してみましょう。本文を見ずに、上のキーワードを参考にしたり、本文の表現を思い出したりしながら自分の言葉で話しましょう。

Van Gogh's Period in Arles, France

As a young artist, van Gogh decided to move to Arles, seeking a new life.

画風について In Arles, thanks to _____

_____, van Gogh began to _____

_____.

共同生活の始まり He invited _____

_____.

Van Gogh decided to _____.

Unit 15

What's in a Name?

音読POINT 複雑な文構造を読む

Picture Dictionary

DL 159 　CD2-69

日本語を参考に空所に入る語を選択肢から選び、イラストの説明を完成させましょう。

1.

A snow-capped mountain _____ from a train（車窓から見える雪山）

2.

Mr. McKinley, the 25th _____ of the US（第25代米国大統領、マッキンリー氏）

3.

_____ to the mountain as Denali（その山をデナリと呼ぶ）

4.

Campaign to have the name changed _____（名前を元に戻す運動を起こす）

| refer | president | seen | back |

Fact Checker

これは北米大陸でもっとも高い山の説明です。音声を聞き、空所に当てはまる語を書き入れましょう。

Denali (previously referred to as Mt. McKinley)

- **Location** South-central ¹A_____
- **Height**   20,310 feet (6,190 meters) above ²s_____ level
- **Name**   Denali (meaning "The Great One" in the ³I_____ language, or just "high," according to some linguists)
- **You Should Know** The famous Japanese climber Naomi Uemura lost his life on Denali in 1984, after reaching the ⁴p_____.

Note linguist「言語学者」

Try!

次の各語句のもっとも強く発音される部分に印をつけましょう。その後、ペアになって1～3を交互に音読しましょう。

1. Denali   2. Mt. McKinley   3. Alaska

Reading-Aloud Warm-Up

次の文は、2015年にオバマ元大統領が発表したある決断について書かれたものです。ペアになって1人ずつ音読し、相手の読み方と自分の読み方を比べてみましょう。

In September 2015, President Obama announced that he had decided to change the name back to Denali. The fact that the struggle lasted so long and was so difficult demonstrates powerfully that a name is more than just a word.

Reading

🎧 DL 161~166　💿 CD2-71 ~ 💿 CD2-76

本文を読んで、続く問題に取り組みましょう。

A When you hear the name "Mount Fuji," what do you think of? A majestic snow-capped mountain seen from a speeding Shinkansen train? A woodblock print by Hokusai? Climbing Japan's highest mountain to watch a spectacular sunrise? Famous names awaken many different feelings and images.

B Names are important. They indicate something unique and are also a reflection of history and culture. There is power in a name—and in being able to give one.

C What about America's highest mountain? Until recently, maps showed that it was a mountain called Mt. McKinley, in Alaska. That name was suggested by a supporter of William McKinley, a presidential candidate in the election of 1896. McKinley went on to become the 25th President of the United States, and he was popular enough to be elected to a second term. But in 1901, he was shot dead by an assassin. In 1917, the American government officially confirmed that the mountain was called Mt. McKinley.

D The problem was that people in Alaska itself had always referred to the mountain as "Denali," based on the name given to it by the local Koyukon tribe, who lived just north of the mountain. The mountain had a special place in their culture, and many felt that the federal government had no right to give it a different name. For many years, Alaskans campaigned to have the name changed back to Denali.

E The debate went on for many years, with one side claiming that it was an insult to the local people to ignore the traditional name Denali, and the other side claiming that to get rid of the name Mt. McKinley was an insult to the memory of the assassinated president.

F Finally, however, in September 2015, President Obama announced that he had decided to change the name back to Denali. His decision was a small but important step that recognized the importance of traditional cultures and the rights of local tribes. The fact that the struggle lasted so long and was so difficult demonstrates powerfully that a name is more than just a word.

Notes

woodblock print「版画」 awaken「呼び起こす」 reflection「反映」 elect「選ぶ」 assassin「暗殺者」 confirm「承認する」 the Koyukon tribe「コユーコン族」 the federal government「連邦政府」 claim「主張する」 get rid of「取り去る」 insult to「〜に対する侮辱」 demonstrate「示す」

Check!

本文のパラグラフ A C D E F の内容に合うように、正しい選択肢を選びましょう。

A　有名な名前は [¹ 多くの人の記憶に残る / ² 様々な感情やイメージを呼び起こす / ³ 国の伝統文化と関連がある]。

C　米国でもっとも高い山は、[¹ 米国大統領が名前を付けた / ² 1917年以来名前が変わっていない / ³ 米国政府が公式に名前を付けたことがある]。

D　アラスカの地元の人々は、[¹ デナリ族と呼ばれていた / ² 地元の山を昔から決まった名前で呼んでいた / ³ マッキンリー大統領と関わりが深かった]。

E F　山の呼称問題をめぐる論争に対し、オバマ大統領は [¹ マッキンリーという名前を支持する人々 / ² 地元の人々 / ³ 両方の立場] の主張を尊重する決断を下した。

Repeat and Look Up!

DL 167, 168　CD2-77　CD2-78

以下は本文中の2文です。日本語訳を完成させましょう。
次に教科書を閉じ、音声に続いてフレーズごとに声に出して暗唱しましょう。

1. People in Alaska itself / had always referred to the mountain as "Denali," / based on the name / given to it by the local Koyukon tribe. // (本文 l. 17)
   アラスカの人々は、地元のコユーコン族によって＿＿＿＿＿＿＿＿＿＿＿＿＿
   ＿＿＿＿＿＿＿＿＿＿＿＿＿＿＿＿＿＿＿＿＿＿。

2. Finally, however, / in September 2015, / President Obama announced / that he had decided / to change the name / back to Denali. // (本文 l. 27)
   しかし、ついに2015年の9月、＿＿＿＿＿＿＿＿＿＿＿＿＿＿＿＿＿＿＿
   ＿＿＿＿＿＿＿＿＿＿＿＿＿＿宣言しました。

Reading Aloud

デナリの呼称をめぐる論争の結論について書かれたパラグラフ F を音読してみましょう。

1. まず太字で示された強く読む部分と 音読POINT の文に注意しながら、パラグラフ F を聞きましょう。
   次に、自分でも / と ⌣ の記号（詳細は p.6）を書き込んでみましょう。

   DL 169   CD2-79

Finally, how**ev**er, in Sep**tem**ber **2015**, **Pre**sident O**ba**ma an**nounced** that he had de**cid**ed to **change** the **name back** to De**na**li. His de**ci**sion was a **small** but im**por**tant **step** that rec**og**nized the im**por**tance of tra**di**tional **cul**tures and the **rights** of local **tribes**.　音読POINT　[The **fact** / that the **strug**gle **last**ed **so long** / and was **so difficult**] / **dem**onstrates **pow**erfully / that a **name** is / **more** than **just** a **word**. //

音読POINT　複雑な文構造を読む

ポイント文は主部が demonstrates の前までと長いので、途中でポーズを入れて構いませんが、主部のまとまりを意識して読みましょう。文全体では、目的語にあたる that a name is...の直前のポーズが一番長くなるように読みます。that a name is...以下は少し速度を落として、太字の語を 1 つずつ大切に読むと引き締まった印象を与えることができます。

---

2. 最後に、ペアになって上の英文を1人ずつ音読し、*Check Points!* をもとに評価しあいましょう。

☑ *Check Points!*
❶ 強弱を意識し、リズムに乗って読めているか　　　　　　　　　　　　[　　／3点]
❷ 書き込んだ通りにポーズ、音のつながりを意識して読めているか　　　[　　／3点]
❸ ポイント文について、音読POINT を意識して読めているか　　　　　　[　　／3点]

Total Score:　／9点

Retelling the Story

デナリとアラスカの人々との関わりについて、自分の言葉で再現してみましょう。

1. まずパラグラフ D をもう一度聞き、下のイラストに関連するキーワードを書き込んでみましょう。

   DL 170   CD2-80

▶ Key Words
(   )

▶ Key Words
(   )

2. 次に、下の英文の下線部を補いながら、デナリとアラスカの人々の関わりを、以下の2つの点に沿って説明しましょう。本文を見ずに、上のキーワードを参考にしたり、本文の表現を思い出したりしながら自分の言葉で話しましょう。

Denali: A Special Place for People in Alaska

山の呼称について　People in Alaska always _____
_____ .

The mountain _____ .

人々の主張　Many felt that the government _____
_____ . For many years, Alaskans _____
_____ .

本書には CD（別売）があります

Pleasure in Reading Aloud and Retelling
音読とリテリングのための 15 話

2019 年 1 月 20 日　初版第 1 刷発行
2025 年 2 月 20 日　初版第 9 刷発行

著　者　　Anthony P. Newell
　　　　　山　口　高　領

発行者　　福　岡　正　人
発行所　　株式会社　金　星　堂
（〒101-0051）東京都千代田区神田神保町 3-21
　　　　　Tel.（03）3263-3828（営業部）
　　　　　　　（03）3263-3997（編集部）
　　　　　Fax（03）3263-0716
　　　　　https://www.kinsei-do.co.jp

編集担当／蔦原美智　　　　　　　　　　　　Printed in Japan
印刷所／日新印刷株式会社　製本所／松島製本
本書の無断複製・複写は著作権法上での例外を除き禁じられています。本書を代行業者等の第三者に依頼してスキャンやデジタル化することは、たとえ個人や家庭内での利用であっても認められておりません。
落丁・乱丁本はお取り替えいたします。

ISBN978-4-7647-4083-9　　　　C1082